JESUS KILLED MY CHURCH

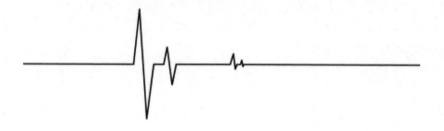

RANDY BOHLENDER

Destiny Image₍ₐ₎ Publishers, Inc.
PO Box 310, Shippensburg, PA 17257-0310
"Promoting Inspired Lives."

ISBN 10 digit: 0-7684-0319-7
ISBN 13 digit: 978-0-7684-0319-0

For Worldwide DistributionPrinted in the U.S.A.

This book and all other Destiny Image, Revival Press, MercyPlace, Fresh Bread, Destiny Image Fiction, and Treasure House books are available at Christian bookstores and distributors worldwide.

For a U.S. bookstore nearest you, call 1-800-722-6774.Or reach us on the Internet: www.destinyimage.com.

1 2 3 4 5 6 7 / 16 15 14 13 12

Dedicated to my dear wife, Kelsey.

I am eternally grateful for your love,
your fearlessness, and your huge prophetic sail.
Let's start something. What could happen?

ACKNOWLEDGMENTS

A special thank you to Adam and Melody Mosley and our whole SpiritLife family. Your graciousness in difficult times was a gift to us.

I'm grateful for Steve Sjogren, Mike Bickle and Lou Engle. You three form an unlikely triumvirate that has shaped my thinking for the last decade. Together, you convinced me the best is yet to come.

Thank you to my children, Jackson, Grayson, Zion, Zoe, Anna, Mercy, Piper, Creed, and Cadence. You have obliterated boredom in my life.

I'm also thankful for our supporters who continue to enable us to minister in the House of Prayer and partner with God to set the lonely in families through adoption. We do this together.

Thank you to those who pre-ordered this project to enable us to produce it debt free. Especially Adam Mosley, Mitch Yap, Nate Hagerty, Charlie Pharis, Matt Beer, and Mike and Janice Yeager, who contributed sacrificially.

CONTENTS

ONE

Perfect Timing

—⚬—

Most of my writing projects start with a story. Or a very vague idea. I rarely see the fullness of a thought from the front end—I have to begin to talk my way into it, through it and out the backside. Even when it's finished, I rarely know what to call it. Strangely, in the very early, early stages of this project—before words fell to the page in rough notes—I had a title.

You have to understand, historically I have resisted titling things. It's never felt right to me; but in this case, I liked the title. It was easy to remember and summarized the whole of what I was trying to say.

What I didn't realize was that the title was polarizing and catalytic. People reacted to the simple, four-word sentence, albeit in radically different ways. Some chuckled. Others rolled their eyes. Some found it incendiary, as they raised an eyebrow and asked in a harsh tone, "Are you saying He wants to kill mine?" A few quietly whispered, "He killed mine too..."

Does Jesus want to kill your church? I have no idea.

Frankly, this book isn't about your church...or at least, not in my mind. Perhaps it is in yours. This isn't a template for what God wants to do in your specific congregation. It's a set of reflections on what He did in our situation and what my take-aways were from that experience. If some find meaning for their own story in mine, that's a wonderful thing. At the same time, if some reject my story out of fear that it will become theirs, I would hope they just read it quietly, in the dark of night if necessary, with an open heart. I'd rather you learn at my expense than your own. I've already paid for the lessons.

I've always found it helpful to interpret my own story in retrospect rather than in real time. In the moment, while the feelings are the strongest, they're often the least balanced. I cannot react with Spock-like coolness to the sting of rejection, or even the insincere praise of men. It takes me awhile to internalize, reflect, pray, and feel things accurately. This sort of processing has served me well. Knowing how I am wired, God has always provided me with milestones, so that I can glance over my shoulder and see in retrospect what I could not see in the moment.

This book is about what I could not see in the moment. It's about learning to live with disappointment, trusting God's sovereignty, and believing that He meant it when He said He works all things together for good. My journey to this perspective did not happen overnight, or even in one extended season, but rather in a series of moments that collectively changed the way I think about the past.

One Christmas Eve we went to the prayer room as we try to do for a while each Christmas Eve. We are part of a community of believers who maintain a 24/7 prayer and worship meeting. For more than eleven years, instrumentalists and intercessors have played, sung, and prayed the Scriptures through the day and night. It's hard to explain the value of cumulative prayer, but it makes for a sacred space.

It's a wonderful place on that holy evening—often fairly empty, one musician and a scattering of people singing a song for a Savior on the night we remember His birth. I'd like to tell you how in tune I was with the majesty of it, but I was in my nearly annual funk a day or two early.

Most years between Christmas and New Year, I would dip into a mild depression. It's not the dark night of the soul. It's more like the frustrated spot of the middle-aged guy. The spot would take a few variations from year to year, but it revolved around this thought: Am I happy with what I've accomplished this year? And invariably, year after year, I wasn't. Going into each winter, I approached the end of the year with a jumble of unrealized expectations, and the knowledge that they were unrealized largely because I had fallen short of my own goals. I'd start staring off into space around Thanksgiving, and by the time I hit late December I was overwhelmed with a hodgepodge of would've, should've, could've thoughts weighing on me. Whatever I'd done any given year, it was never enough.

The needle of the soul-o-meter was dipping left that evening as I faced the ending of another year that didn't turn out like I'd hoped. The book that I'd talked so much about writing was not yet published, or even started, for that matter. We were selling our house, but the house we were buying was in unlivable condition, having been empty for years. As a result, we were staying in a borrowed house, and it would be many cold, dark months before we would walk into our own home. I had transitioned from a significant role in a ministry to what felt like a hanger-on, the team member who would not go away but didn't really have any authority or duties either. A good bit of my identity had been stripped away that year, and while I felt I knew who I was, I also believed I was the only person on earth who did.

I felt dislocated, unknown, tired, and more than a little sorry for myself. Okay, a lot sorry for myself.

As I stood to the side of the prayer room, holding my three-month-old daughter, my back against the wall in more ways than one, I got gut-level honest with the Lord. Whispering my confession in prayer, I told Him everything. "I'm not happy with what I've done this year...I'm so disappointed. I'm so disappointed."

I looked down for a moment at Anna, asleep in my arms. She was completely unaware of the wrenching of my soul. She had three concerns in life—a clean diaper, a warm place to sleep, and a bottle. Presently I was meeting two of those three and I could pull a bottle out of the diaper bag if necessary. She was perfectly content.

In a moment, I heard the Whisper. I've heard it before. I actually think it speaks quite often, but I'm usually too busy to take notice. It's not an audible voice, though I'd love it to be. Though technically silent, it echoed within me.

"I know you're not happy with what you've done this year."

I had to confess I was not, although God knowing this was not necessarily a sign of omniscience on His part. Anyone who's ever taken a sophomore college class on body language could tell by the slump of my shoulders that this was not an up moment for me.

The Whisper reiterated, **"I know you're not happy with what you've done this year...but what do you think about what I've done?"**

What followed was a palpable, awkward silence. I was troubled by this statement, but too smart to answer quickly. The Voice was comfortable with the silence—He had no compulsion to say any more. He could say more with silence than I could with all the words in the world. What did I think about what He had done this year? He had enjoyed a very good year.

I glanced down at my gorgeous daughter, a perfect Japanese-Thai-Caucasian blend, and then across the room at her twin sister in her mother's arms. Hot tears began to drop down off my checks onto her blanket. The memories of adopting the twins began to swirl through my head, followed by a myriad of things that His hand had done in the past year. Babies born. Friendships formed. Vision dropping like stars into our dreams at night.

Then it hit me. We didn't do everything we wanted to this year, but He certainly did everything He wanted.

We often measure the seasons in our life by what we hoped for, what we did, what we failed to do, and whether or not our plan worked. Especially in ministry, with souls on the line, being less than the stellar success that we prayed for, hoped for, and budgeted for seems like failure more bitter than death. This sort of thinking strips away the sovereignty of God and places every hope for success and blame for failure on what we could not possibly accomplish. It also misses the point that God is always at work, even in our shortcomings. Even in our supposed failures. It fails to acknowledge that our failings are the rich seedbed of opportunity for His greatness to be revealed.

That fateful Christmas Eve, even standing in the prayer room holding my daughter, I was so consumed with what I wanted to do and didn't that I was looking past His rich leadership and provision in my life. I was right that a book had not been written, but I had two daughters who were not on my radar, my master plan, or my to-do list the previous January. We adopted them in a whirlwind thirty-six hour adventure that I've outlined in a prior book, *The Spirit of Adoption*. It was a miracle—everyone said so, and we knew it to be true. Nevertheless I had stumbled through a year thinking I was missing the mark, while God was at work revealing His true purpose for this season. I was grousing about missing a writing deadline, and God had granted me authority and responsibility for two human souls that would never die. I'd missed more than a writing deadline—I'd missed what God was doing entirely.

I vowed that night that I wouldn't live another year like the last. If the hand of God was at work in all things, then I wanted to learn to see the hand day by day. I wanted to train myself to perceive Him in real time, even when things didn't go as I planned. I wanted to live with a grateful heart, knowing that the summary of my life would not be what I did but rather what He did in my proximity, which I could neither cause nor thwart.

God is forever writing our story, and He gives us the dignity of being able to introduce characters that occasionally wrinkle, but not alter, the plot. Often we think we've done something that permanently changes the trajectory of what might have been if we'd only been more obedient or pious. He smiles at this. He knows how many pages He has left before He needs to bring resolve, and He knows that it's going to be okay.

Further complicating things, God rarely writes in a linear fashion. Linear stories that move from character introduction to conflict to resolution in less than thirty minutes are products of a television generation. Real life—God life—doesn't work that way. Characters step on stage or fall off stage at inopportune times. It often seems that there are more twists than plot. At times, we think we're living a two hour movie, only to find out it's a mini series. More often than not, we're not even able to articulate the conflict accurately because of our own misperceptions of the situation. Yet God continues to write, all the while developing characters around us and character within us.

I'm going to save you a little thinking and give you a few indicators of what you'll discover about me in this book.

In the moment, I rarely fully know what God is doing. I try—really, I do—but I'm almost incapable of stepping back and seeing the long view that God takes. His answers are always more complicated, more magnificent, and more character-building than I would have expected (and sadly, often more character building than I would have chosen). Nevertheless, just because I can't always perceive what God is doing at the moment doesn't mean I can't see His hand in the past, and use that information to reconcile my expectations with my reality.

While much of my family's story feels like random chance, God focused on moving people and events in a manner that seemed like a model to test an elaborate chaos theory. Chaos theory is the idea that the smallest event in a complex system can significantly alter big events far from the original happening. The classic illustration is a butterfly flapping its wings in China and starting a chain of events that results in a hurricane off the coast of Florida.

We erroneously believe that life simply happens to us and God helps us cope like some supernatural responder to the Serenity Prayer. God isn't just in the coping business. He is in control of everything. He utilizes what feels like small and insignificant things far from us to start people and resources into movement, only to reach us at our specific moment in need. We wonder if help is coming at all—and little do we know that the help has already been set in motion. If only we could learn to trust for the help before we see it.

A few years ago, some bad planning and confusing tax laws for ministers left us in the strange position of having had a low income and incredibly high tax burden. I am reticent to even mention the specifics, because everyone's idea of "high tax burden" is somewhat different, but the number was significant enough that it bears mentioning. When April 15th rolled around, we owed $9,700.

We were stunned. At the time, we had four children and a meager income. We swallowed hard, looked at the bill, scrounged up every dollar we had, and subtracted. It left about $9,700. It wasn't that we couldn't pay it all—we couldn't pay any of it! We did what every good red-blooded American might do. We filed an extension and started to pray.

The extension gave us until October 15th of that year. We felt that surely something would break before then. We were so confident that I don't remember praying about it much until late that summer, when October 15th seemed just around the corner. Into September, I grew very spiritual, praying more and more and more. I reminded God that we needed it, reminded Him that we were His children, and reminded Him that if we were to end up on the street eating Funyons, it was going to be a poor reflection on Him as a father. All these prayers gained me nothing but stress.

By September 15th, I was no longer the mighty man of faith and power. I was a wreck. For the next week I didn't eat much, I couldn't sleep, and I agonized in prayer. I remember specifically praying that mantra prayer of the lost cause: "Oh God, Oh God, Oh God." It turns out He actually hears that prayer.

On September 22nd, around 11 a.m., I was in the prayer room sweating bullets. I was pacing. I was praying. I was pleading and interceding. Suddenly, I heard the Lord in a way I had not in a long time—certainly not in relation to this issue. I heard His voice resound in my spirit. Often we've said, "We'd do anything just to hear one word from the Lord..." and I did.   He said, **"Stop."** I immediately stopped, but it was more out of perplexity than any sort of obedience.

"Stop?" I thought. "What could that mean?" The first thing that came to mind was Occam's Razor. First year philosophy students will remember Occam's Razor as a philosophical axiom. It declares that "given a multitude of solutions, the simplest is most commonly correct." I applied this axiom and came to reason that the Lord was telling me...stop. So I did. I drove home from the prayer meeting and told Kelsey, "The Lord spoke—and He told me to stop asking. My assumption is that He's got it taken care of." It should be noted that there was nothing concrete to indicate this was true—only the word "stop."

A week later, I received a card from a long-time friend in another city. It read, "Dear Randy and Kelsey, I'm writing to tell you that we are sending a check along shortly. Recently our son was hospitalized. When the bill arrived, I opened it and began to thank the Lord that we had good health insurance. The Lord spoke to me and told me to send the amount of the bill to a missionary who may not have any..."

Kelsey and I began to rejoice, even as we wondered, "Uh, how much?" Days went by with no word. Then October 2nd, we got an email telling us to expect the check to come from a specific entity. It also said, "It will be in the amount of $10,000 and arrive in two to two and a half weeks." We rejoiced—but started counting days. The IRS commitment was due the 15th. The check was scheduled to arrive between the 16th and the 20th. We were not sure that the IRS would be so understanding.

Miraculously, October 8th, the $10,000 check arrived. It cleared our bank on October 15th. We wrote a $9,700 check to the IRS and another for $250 to the tax preparer, and raced them both to the post office. Later we noticed in the bank paperwork that accompanied the check was a notation that it had been ordered on September 22nd—the very day that the Lord had told me to stop.

God, in His infinite wisdom, set the perfect storm in motion, like a butterfly flapping its wings in China might cause a storm in the Caribbean. He sent a hospital bill to a woman who did not need to pay it, on the exact day that it needed to speak to her about giving finances to us in order that it could make its way through the byzantine banking system to hit our bank and be available on the day we would need it. The fact that He spoke the word "stop" to me was simply the icing on the cake. He didn't want His children to concern themselves one day too long. He had it under control, even when the entire situation looked out of control.

Situations like this have built my faith in God's leadership, even when I wasn't sure what He was doing. Even once we knew the money was coming, we weren't sure it would arrive in time. From beginning to end, it would have been easy to wonder if even Jesus knew what He was up to. It was all too nerve wracking to possibly be God's perfect plan. If deliverance is coming, what possible advantage would there be in it coming later? Why not now?

You may be reading this, politely nodding, and muttering, "Yes, yes, great story...but when did Jesus kill your church?"

That will come in subsequent chapters. Before you can even begin to think about Jesus killing your church, you have to believe that Jesus' timing, will, actions, and favor are in remarkable synchronicity with His master plan. He doesn't do anything—promote or demote, give increase or take back—without it fitting exactly into history where He wants it, at a strategic place where He's working for our good.

Trust me. I'm speaking from experience. If He kills your church, His timing will be perfect.

TWO

An Uncomfortable Position

—⚏—

I recently listened to a podcast from *The Moth*, a storytelling series based in New York. It featured Reverend Al Sharpton, the notoriously outspoken civil rights activist, relaying the story of what he referred to as his "calling to care for the underprivileged." As he relayed it, he was a renown "boy preacher" as a child, often winning oratory contests and preaching in churches. At one point, an elder minister gently challenged Sharpton, asking him to decide if he was "called to preach or just gifted." Later, when visiting a man who had stabbed him in a demonstration, Sharpton surprised himself by finding it in his heart to forgive the man. He marks that moment as his moment of "calling" to defend the rights of others. Admittedly, Sharpton and I would differ on a myriad of opinions, but he is a master storyteller, and his fifteen minutes on stage at *The Moth* were spellbinding.

I just don't believe the premise.

As much as we would like to tell others about our burning bush moment, most of us are not Moses. While all believers are called into ministry of some form or another, very few get that life-defining encounter featuring a physical manifestation of God, choirs of angels singing, and a moment in time that we can point to, like 4:12 a.m., Tuesday, August 9, as a moment of calling. Most of us bounce toward our calling like a drunk's bowling ball, hoping to avoid the gutters on either side. When we get where we were going, we're as surprised as everyone else who cheered us along the way, even as they wondered what might happen to us.

I didn't have the burning bush experience. I didn't even have the Al Sharpton experience. I have my experience—just as you are having yours—and I said "have" because in many ways it's still in development. I am doing what God has called me to do—but I've walked with Him long enough to suspect that He's not led me past the last marker on the trail, and there's likely a few sharp turns to come. Knowing so little in advance is actually good for me. It encourages me not to get too far ahead of Him.

My sense of calling goes back to childhood, but it certainly began to congeal my final year of Bible college. After graduating high school, I'd started at Trinity Bible College, a small school in Ellendale, North Dakota. The middle of my sophomore year, I transferred to Central Bible College in Springfield, Missouri.

Transferring in to a small school has its own unique challenges. In these institutions, it really is a four-year experience, and bonds form the freshman year that chart the course for life and ministry. As a transfer student, I wasn't in one of those groups. There was no sort of concerted rejection by others. In fact, the students and professors were very kind. Nevertheless, starting midstream left me feeling somewhat "other than" those around me, and the next year and a half of my college career consisted mostly of my books and a part-time job. Then, the fall of my senior year, everything changed.

I'd returned from an internship in Iowa, ready to finish my degree and get on with ministry, even though I had little idea of what that would look like. Given the loneliness I'd experienced the past year and a half, I was probably more interested in closing the college door than I was opening the ministry door. I'd determined I was going to keep my head down, finish the job at hand, and move on. The wheels fell off this plan the first weekend of the school year.

Needing a few last minute things, I ran to the mall on a Saturday afternoon. As I rode an escalator from an upper level of the mall to the first floor, I glanced to the right and saw my friend, Julie, standing in a card shop. I waved. She waved. And then she stepped to the right.

Behind Julie stood a vision of loveliness. I will not say it was love at first sight, only because I think love needs to stand the test of time before planting that flag. I will go so far as saying it was intense, extreme like at first sight. I heard my friend Julie say, "Randy, this is my friend, Kelsey..." I'm not sure what she said after that. Her voice faded into "wah, wah, wah..." That's about all I heard from her—or anyone else—in the months to follow.

The fall of my senior year of college was a blur as Kelsey and I met, dated, and became engaged by Christmas. I am not a hard core proponent of quick courtships, but in our case, it worked. At the time of this writing, we have been married nearly 22 years, all of them happily.

Once we had decided to get married, the next question was, "What are we going to do?" I had already been anticipating that question as a college senior. No one asks a freshman what they're going to do, because in most cases, the freshman who thinks he knows what he's going to do is wrong anyway. But seniors are different. Seniors are facing serious decisions, big opportunities, and student loans. They are expected to know stuff and do things. Seniors with a wedding on the horizon are under a double amount of expectation.

Even though we both were full-time students and worked part-time, we found hours each week to be together, working to plan our wedding and often, pondering the future. We knew we wanted to be involved in ministry. We also couldn't imagine ourselves pastoring. Neither of us were from pastors' homes—meaning we didn't have strong attachments for or against the idea of taking a church—but we felt deep in our hearts that there was something else that we would do.

I do remember having strong impressions at the time about conventional ministry. In retrospect, I recognize them as having been from the Lord, although at the time I was not as certain of when and where I was hearing His voice, so I filed them under "impressions."

One was that ministry—especially preaching, as it was being done in our sphere—was significantly disconnected from people. Our Bible college was located in the city that also hosted the headquarters for our denomination. As a result, there were a plethora of churches of our tribe sprinkled across the city, many of them flagship churches for the organization. To be clear, these were good churches full of godly people and pastored by great, godly men. Nevertheless, as I sat Sunday after Sunday and listened to remarkable orators, I couldn't help but notice how little of what they said would have been understood by the non-Christian college students who I worked with at my part-time job, in the back office of a large retail store. It pained me that these churches, keepers of the greatest message of all time, were communicating it in such a way that the friends I worked with would probably never understand.

I remember spending an hour in prayer with Kelsey in the school chapel one afternoon and being tormented by this thought. I was strongly impressed that the communication of the gospel was going to take unique forms in the years to come—it had to because it was the most important message in the world, and Jesus would find a way.

As I walked back and forth among the seats, crying out to God, I had a thought: One day, pastors would preach the gospel and refer to current events, going so far as using video clips from CNN and other current references. They would teach about Israel using real-time examples and projecting those examples on big screens behind them. Of course, at the time, most of the larger churches in America were using overhead projectors, and this being twenty years prior to YouTube or Hulu, even if they had had the wherewithal to project video easily there would have been no way to capture the video clips. It was an idea ahead of its time—but God's ideas are often revealed ahead of time to put a fire in us to pray. I think I shared my idea with Kelsey that afternoon, but no one else. Years later, when this very thing began to happen, I couldn't help but think back to that afternoon.

My second impression was related to our future. As friends began to receive invitations to pastor or youth pastor at churches across the nation, much was made among my classmates—myself included—regarding "finding a position." I cringe when I reflect on referring to taking a ministry role as "finding a position," but that's what many of us were looking for—a position that would legitimize our education and calling. Our version of the question about a tree falling in the woods with no one to hear it was, "If a Bible college graduate preaches in the woods and no one listens, was he ever called?" Having just dispatched my primary fear in life—that I would never find a wife—I attacked my secondary fear—that I would never find a position, and that we would stumble into married life wondering how we got to be adults with no apparent value to the world.

Long hours were spent talking with Kelsey about what sort of position we wanted. We were both reticent to pastor, but most young ministers didn't become pastors right away anyhow. Most take roles as staff pastors for a season, finishing their education at the School of Hard Knocks before being fully unleashed on an unsuspecting congregation.

I do remember a word coming up repeatedly in conversation: unconventional. We wanted to do ministry in a way we weren't seeing it done in our circles, although we couldn't articulate what we were imagining. It's fun, in retrospect, to think about those days in light of how the Lord has led us, but in the moment it wasn't fun. Having spent four years in training for something specific,

I found myself suddenly at odds with the specifics of what I was trained for. My heart was set toward ministry, yet the only models I had been exposed to were ones that I had no deep interest in investigating.

The spring semester weeks wore on. We landed a wedding day – July 7th. We found a church for the wedding—a large sanctuary on the north side of Cincinnati where Kelsey had gone to church during her high school years. One thing remained nagging at us. Once we were married, what would we do?

When you're twenty-one years old and dreaming about doing things in an unconventional way but have no real experience, it's easy to return to the conventional way of doing things. By mid-semester, I'd postponed my idealism and started searching the "Help Wanted" board outside the Dean of Students' office. Almost immediately, I discovered a church a few hours away that was looking for a youth pastor. I made a phone call, mailed a short resume (anything over half a page would have involved serious creative writing skills), and quickly received an invitation to come for a visit—along with my wife-to-be.

Twenty-plus years later, I can honestly say I have almost no memory of the next few weeks. I remember vaguely staying at a host home. I remember visiting the church. They must have asked questions and we must have answered them, because at some point shortly thereafter, we were asked to join the church staff (or be the church staff, to be more accurate) after graduation. I remember telling them yes. I remember my fiancé's perplexed look, and her saying something like, "This feels weird." What I distinctly remember is that we didn't pray much about it. I made a decision based almost entirely on my need.

Every other weekend after that decision was made until I graduated from college, Kelsey and I would make the three hour drive to the church. Those weekends were busy with meeting people, getting to know the pastor, and holding a Saturday night youth service. In a precursory demonstration of my leadership skills, the youth group quickly grew from ten to three. I'm not sure where the other seven went. In reality, they may never have existed—but we were told they were out there and would certainly return (they did not). I'm actually convinced the three who remained did so under order of their parents. It wasn't because they were being led well. Understand, I was doing the best I knew how, it's just that how I knew wasn't very good. The great diaspora happened before graduation, so we told ourselves that things would get better when we moved there full-time. This ended up being a sort of coping mechanism at the time, although it was quickly revealed to have no basis in reality.

After graduation, we moved to the small town. Kelsey stayed with a host family and I rented a room in a house owned by one of the board members. We left town for two weeks to get married and then returned to a little house on the edge of town to set up housekeeping.

In short order, tension began to grow with the host family, I began to suspect the board member whose house I was living in of having an extramarital affair (later proved right) and I found myself at odds with the pastor on a number of decisions. Even at the time, I knew that the decisions that he and I were differing on were not deal breakers. They were not issues of doctrine or morality. They were leadership differences that might have been surmountable had I been emotionally vested, or felt a more distinct sense of calling to the city, but I wasn't.

After trying for months to navigate the difficulties, I phoned a trusted advisor who pointedly asked me, "Do you want to stay?" I had to admit that I didn't want to stay—we'd talked about leaving a number of times. He challenged, "If your heart isn't in it, and you're not happy there, quit now. If you don't, you'll end up staying several years and leave anyway, breaking their hearts and yours too. If you're going, go now."

We announced our resignation to the pastor a few days later. I got the distinct feeling he was more relieved than frustrated. It may be that he and I both learned a lesson about praying before making big hiring decisions. Whatever the case, we quietly prepared to move on...except that we had no place to move on to. Having no options, we decided to go to North Dakota and live with my parents for a season.

For all our worry about "finding a position" before graduating from Bible college, I was now four months out of Bible college, married, having resigned my first job in ministry, and moving my new bride back to my parents' farm in rural North Dakota. This was not the glorious introduction to ministry that I had imagined for so many years.

My parents drove down to help us move. We loaded what little furniture we had onto a flatbed trailer, which my father pulled behind his pickup truck. Kelsey and I drove separate cars the 900 miles north, stopping periodically to let our little dog stretch her legs. Every time we had a moment to talk privately, we would ask each other the same question: "What do you want to do?" It was like we were both eight years old, standing on the corner of the playground and looking at the equipment. "What do you want to do?" I didn't have an answer. All I could remember was the deep and earnest desire to do something unconventional.

At one point, my mom volunteered to drive one of our cars, so Kelsey and I enjoyed a few hundred miles together in her old battered Celica. Again, the conversation started.

"What should we do now?" Kelsey asked.

"I don't know. What do you want to do?" I said. Kelsey is a visionary. She has always had what I call a large prophetic sail. She can feel the wind of the Lord on something long before I do. Feeling a bit of that wind, she began to speak, slowly but with great conviction.

"I want to live in a big house, with a bunch of teenagers, and teach them about Jesus, and disciple them, and help them get their lives together."

I was silent for a moment. As gifted as Kelsey is at hearing the Lord, I have a gift set of my own. One of my strongest gifts is the ability to see the hole in the problem from a mile away. Some people call it being negative. I prefer to think of it as discernment. The truth is probably somewhere in the middle. Call it gifting or negative thinking, I had to respond.

"Kelsey, that's great. Really, it is. But that sort of place doesn't exist. And if it does...if there is a home somewhere where teenagers are discipled and taught about Jesus and helped with getting their life together, you ought to be in the home, not running the home, because you're nineteen years old!"

The rest of the ride home was very cold, inside the car and out. In my urgency to lead my wife to realism, I'd squashed her dream. I regretted it the moment I did it, but words spoken are difficult to rescind. She was not angry, but she needed time to process. And I needed time to ask God to forgive me for speaking so quickly.

Fortunately for both of us, she is the resilient sort, because she recovered from my unsolicited input. Her gift of dreaming the dreams of God, out loud, has served us well in subsequent decades. At the time, though, I couldn't have anticipated just how well it would serve us. And I certainly couldn't have anticipated how quickly her words would ring true.

THREE

Eight is Enough

—ɯ—

After two days of driving, we turned east off of Highway 41 onto a gravel county road that stretched a half mile to where the county deemed it no longer necessary to maintain. From there, it was just another quarter mile north on a private driveway to the farm where I had grown up.

From the moment we left the highway, every detail was familiar to me. Before leaving to go to college, it was the only home I'd ever known. When I was born, I was brought home from the hospital to this house. I'd known boyhood, adolescence, and my teen years on this ten acre yard and the accompanying 150 acres of farm land. Now, I was facing it as a young man with a wife.

There's something humbling about going back to where you started in a way you didn't intend. In all our years of working with young people, I don't think I ever heard one say, "I hope to get an education, get married and move back in with mom and dad." It's just not done.

As strange as my reentry to this world was, it was Kelsey's first entry. She had visited with me twice before we were married, for a few days each time, but now we were driving in with suitcases and boxes packed. We didn't know if this was for a week, a month, or a year. To be honest, we would never have verbalized that it could be longer than a month or two, but deep in our hearts, we were both probably worried that it might stretch out longer than we anticipated.

Now, firmly ensconced in our upstairs bedroom, we began to pray and think about our next step. I worked on stretching my resume past a half page and Kelsey took a job at a local Christian bookstore while adjusting to in-laws who put butter on their ham sandwhiches and had no grid for her city upbringing. I felt like a strange, ministerial version of Eddie Albert, who had dragged his city wife to the country for a remake of Green Acres.

The second week we were in North Dakota, our denomination was holding its annual ministers' retreat. The three day event was an opportunity for pastors across the state to worship, receive training, and spend hours together with people who had similar hurts and victories. Kelsey and I weren't exactly likely candidates to attend, given that we'd just moved into the state and hadn't had enough ministry experience to warrant any kind of retreat, but I knew this event was more than just a retreat. It was a networking opportunity.

In a moment of uncharacteristic boldness, I called the state-wide denominational leader and gave him the ninety second version of our story. I didn't whitewash it, I simply explained that we'd taken a role prematurely and were really looking for what God might have for us. He interrupted my hamfisted attempt at an introduction and said "Randy, I want you to come with your wife to the retreat this weekend."

I told him that we'd love to do that, but we really didn't have the registration fee. "No need to worry," he told us, "You will be taken care of."

A few days later, in a hotel conference room with fifty or sixty other pastors and their wives, the denomination's leader who had invited us asked us to stand. He then gave a heartfelt pitch for anyone who might be looking for a staff member to please consider this wonderful couple. It was one of the strongest endorsements I've ever received in ministry—something that continues to amuse me because, to my knowledge, our conversation a few days prior was the only time we had ever talked in our lives.

Immediately following the meeting, a man made his way across the room to meet us. As he shook our hands, he told us, "Our church is looking for a youth pastor, and you two may be exactly what we need." He gave me a business card and shook our hands. I tucked the card in my pocket, thinking how great it was that the Lord would open doors like this. Kelsey, on the other hand, winced a little. Her memory was better than mine, and she remembered that just two weeks ago we'd resigned a similar position because we weren't any good at it.

As the pastor walked away, another couple approached us. The husband, a distinguished man with a resonate voice, quickly told us, "We're not pastors...but we direct a foundation that maintians two homes for troubled teens in Williston, North Dakota. Currently, we have an opening in the boys' home. We need a couple to live in a big house with a bunch of teenagers, and teach them about Jesus, and disciple them, and help them get their lives together. Might you be interested?"

Kelsey's hand had been resting on my arm. Instantly it squeezed tight, threatening to cut off the circulation of blood to my forearm. This man's description of the opportunity was exactly what Kelsey had said as we drove to North Dakota a few weeks before...the exact thing that I told Kelsey "doesn't exist."

"We're interested," I said, trying to disguise the fact that I was near fainting because of the uncanny similarities to my wife's earlier desire.

"Great. Let's have breakfast tomorrow and talk," he said. With that, we set a time to meet and parted ways. That night, lying in our bed in that little upstairs bedroom of the farm house, we could hardly sleep. Could it be that God had been speaking to Kelsey so that we would be ready for this opportunity when it afforded itself? Sadly, our ministerial training had given us a lot of theology but not a lot of practical experience, especially in hearing God's voice. We weren't sure if this was God or a cruel trick, but we knew we had to walk it out.

The next morning, we met with them. Immediately we hit it off. His dry sense of humor meshed with mine. His wife was from Ohio and, like Kelsey, felt a little like someone who had moved to the moon when she moved to North Dakota. By the time the second cup of coffee had been poured, I think we all knew where this was headed.

He described the home in great detail. It was privately funded by a Christian couple, who had left their estate to the establishment of two homes for teens. Residents were placed there by the court, but being a private establishment, they had a fair amount of freedom in what they were able to say about the Lord. Residents went to church and public school, all the while working themselves up through a series of levels with graduated degrees of freedom and responsibility. Upon leaving the home, most of them went back to their parents. While no work of this kind is fail-safe, this group did have a remarkable rate of success—so much that the state would send workers to study how things were done in hopes of replicating their success. Of course, in replicating the program minus Jesus, they were never able to get it right. There were a lot of places in the state where a wayward teen could get a warm bed and a balanced meal. There were few places where that same kid could get a clear, relationship-based presentation of the gospel, but when they did, God broke in and made a difference.

We left the meeting stirred at the possibilities. This was very different from youth pastoring. It was different from anything we'd ever considered. It was...unconventional. Later that night, I received a phone call from the director of the home. He wanted to know if we would come to Williston to spend the weekend and interview. I quickly said yes, and once agreeing, I began to wonder how I would explain Williston to my city wife.

As we drove the two hours west to Williston, I started in. "Williston...is a bit of a cow town."

"North Dakota is made up of cow towns," she replied, inferring that if you'd seen one cow town, you'd seen them all.

"Agreed," I said. "But even by cow town standards, Williston is pretty remote."

Kelsey assured me she understood, but as we drove west, through towns spaced 30 or 40 miles apart and decreasing in size, I saw that she began to truly comprehend what she was getting into. Going to Williston would be not unlike going to the ends of the earth for this girl. Having been married only a few months, we were looking at our third move, and each move seemed further and further from how she had grown up.

The weekend interviews covered the gamut. We talked about state law, parenting philosophy, house organization, and everything in between. The morning of the second day, they mentioned that as part of the job, Kelsey would be the cook for all ten of us—eight boys plus her and I. As part of the interview, Kelsey would need to cook a meal.

There was a small snag. Kelsey had not grown up cooking. In fact, at this point I had known her parents for over a year and spent a fair amount of time with them. Never once had I seen her mother cook anything. Some women reach for a cook book—Kelsey's mom reached for a phone book. They ate take-out nearly every night.

In that moment, when Kelsey was faced with a challenge that she was not prepared for, I watched her do what I've seen her do a hundred times since then: smile, nod, and resolve to figure it out. That afternoon, I watched her in the kitchen as she did what she did not know how to do—cook for eight boys, the two of us, and the director's family of five. A few hours later, the fifteen of us sat down to a delicious meal of stir-fry. As the boys chattered about school, I whispered to Kelsey, "How did you do this?"

"I knew how to make stir fry from reading a recipe," she said. "But the recipe was for a smaller batch, so I just made it really big." Kelsey was made for doing big things, whether it was inspiring others or making stir-fry.

Over the next month, we made two more weekend trips to Williston as part of the interview process. The job involved a lot of responsibility and they wanted to make certain that we were the right people for the job. Later, the director told us that the Lord had spoken to him early in the process and told him we were the people that he was supposed to hire. There was really only one snag: we were younger by ten years than anyone else who had held the role. In fact, at nineteen years of age, Kelsey was only a few months older than some of the boys who were assigned to the home. The director of the home would need to go to the state legislature to get a variance in the state code to allow us to live there, work, and drive the van!

It was early December when we got final word that the job was ours. We were asked to report for work on December 18th. I had promised to take Kelsey home to Cincinnati for Christmas, so we decided to celebrate Christmas early and drove from North Dakota to Ohio to spend two weeks with her parents. Looking back on it, I question our planning skills, because we rolled back into Williston to start our job with only $2 in our pockets and a quarter of a tank of gas in our car. Any time you figure your net worth by factoring how much gas is in your car, you're in dire straits. Even so, we weren't worried, because the perks of our new job included food and housing. We reasoned that we wouldn't need any money until payday on the 31st. Then we remembered that we had three days off between the 18th and 31st. As we unpacked our things, I began to wonder how many packs of Ramen noodles we could buy with $2.

Later that afternoon, our new boss stopped by to ask us to attend the staff Christmas party that night. Exhausted, we dressed up in our finest and went off to meet our new co-workers. I remember trying to find the most direct route to the party and back because after all, we only had a quarter of a tank of gas. Once we were there, we enjoyed a good (free!) dinner and received a card from the board of directors. Once out in the car, we opened the card to discover that for our six hours of faithful service that year, we were given a $100 Christmas bonus.

That incident served as the first of many when the Lord would show Himself to be faithful to us, often at the last minute. It's not that He was late—but rather His timing was perfect so that we needed to recognize His role in it all working out. We could not have orchestrated rolling into town on $2 and a quarter of a tank of gas following a 1,100 mile journey. Our new employers could not have guessed that the latest edition of their team was counting among their biggest assets a few gallons of gas and the cash equivalent of two packs of Ramen noodles. God Himself saw the end from the beginning, and saw fit to stretch us as far as we could be stretched, then graciously make up the gap that we could not fill, with just enough, just in time.

We dove headlong into our roles as houseparents. It required that we do the shopping, the driving, the discipline, and everything else that comes with a house of eight teenage boys. When you add our youth into the mix, it made for interesting dynamics. The first week that we were on duty, the UPS truck pulled up to the house and the delivery man knocked on the door with a package. Kelsey opened the door to receive it, and he refused to give it to her.

"I need to give the box to someone in charge," he said.

Kelsey stifled a laugh and assured him, "Sir, I am in charge. I work here."

He smiled but pressed the issue, "No, who is the houseparent?"

"I really am the houseparent!" she insisted. Finally, when I arrived with several of the boys, all who testified to the fact that yes, this nineteen-year-old girl was in charge, the delivery man sheepishly handed over the package.

The boys who were residents of the home were not really dangerous—in most cases they had been caught after minor brushes with the law. In the investigative process, it became obvious that the parenting they were receiving was contributing to their delinquency. The ultimate goal of the home was to reunite them with their biological parents. It wasn't always easy.

One of our younger guys—I'll call him Chad—was twelve years old. In a house full of braggadocios fifteen- and sixteen-year old-young men, Chad was clearly a boy. He was tender and sensitive, his eyes often filling with tears at the good natured teasing around the kitchen table. He quickly became a favorite of ours—and then we discovered that he was stealing us blind.

We were careful not to leave any objects of value sitting around, but things started disappearing nevertheless...odd objects, like a spatula, or a pencil sharpener. Invariably, they would reappear in Chad's room. Once I caught him stashing six containers of frosting in his heat vent, apparently hoping to steal a cake later and have a party. We would correct him, discipline him, talk him through it, and wait for him to strike again, and he would.

I could never figure out why Chad would steal so blatantly. He never expressed a bit of remorse for it. He would be sorry he got caught, but never sorry about stealing. One day, something he said shed a little light on the situation. We were driving past a farm and Chad told us, "When I lived at home, Mom would take us 'old house hunting.'" Although curiousity was killing me, I'd learned to let the boys talk. I would often learn more by listening than by interrogating. Sure enough, I was not disappointed.

"Old house hunting?" Another boy asked. "What is that?"

Chad lit up at the thought of one of the boys asking him a question. At twelve, he wasn't often considered an authority on much around the house. "You know, old house hunting! It's when you go into one of these old farm houses and find stuff. People move out and leave everything in the homes! Once we found a nice set of dishes, wrapped them up and gave them to my grandma for Christmas!"

The van rolled on in silence for a minute. Finally, one of the older boys said, "Chad, those houses weren't abandoned. Those people were just not home. You weren't hunting anything. Your mom was stealing things from people's houses."

Suddenly, Chad's behavior in the home made sense. He was only acting what he had been taught by his mother—that if a person needed something and they found it unattended, it was theirs to take. That realization led to a series of long conversations about the idea of private property, and how something could belong to someone even if they weren't in the room with the object. All of this was almost a foreign concept to Chad.

I often refer to this season of our lives as a course in leadership and authority. We served at the boy's home for over a year, and in that time I discovered things about myself and others that I may never have learned any other way.

Structure is your friend.

The Boys Home was not a military school, but it did have a sense of order to it. Each morning, Kelsey and I consulted a file box with index cards that kept us on task: when to change the oil in the van, when to mop the entire basement, when to order beef from the butcher. To the uninitiated it might have looked controlling and simplistic, but it meant that things got done on time; and when our day was done, we could go to bed knowing we'd completed our tasks.

That sense of structure was applied to the boys as well. They had twenty minutes to walk the mile to school. That was a steady walk, which kept them out of trouble they would have gotten into if they had another ten minutes on the road. Beds were made daily and rooms kept clean. That eliminated 90 percent of the fights that began with "where is my stuff?"

There is security in discipline.

I did not come from a large family. I had one sister, seven years older than myself, who was killed in a tragic car accident when I was twelve. As a result, I was raised essentially as an only child. A family with one child can live life different from a family with eight. One child getting a little rowdy causes a minor disturbance. Eight rowdy teenagers is a mob scene. If allowed to develop into a mob scene, invariably people would get hurt. Most of them really didn't want a mob either—they just needed to keep up with the others for credibility's sake.

One weekend, my parents came to visit. One of the guys was acting pretty cocky and I'd told him to back off of hassling the others. When he didn't, I assigned him extra chores and told him to sit at the kitchen table until I was ready to talk to him. My dad took me aside and said, "Randy, you're being awfully harsh! We never did that with you!"

I admitted, "You're right, Dad—you didn't. By the time I was seventeen you allowed me to say what I thought I should and act as I thought I should, but I had been trained to speak and act properly. In this case I'm making up for fifteen years of no discipline."

God seeds destiny into our hearts.

Houseparenting at a boys' home was an unusual move for a young couple. It was a major risk for the management of the foundation to take. So much could have gone wrong—but so much went right. It was truly unconventional.

Twenty years later, someone asked me how long we had thought about adopting. I told them we had pondered it for all of our married life. Later, as I mulled the question over in my mind, I realized that even back then, God was sowing seeds in our hearts regarding taking in children. He was allowing us to practice on eight teenagers for the day when we'd have seven children of our own. God was sowing our own destiny, giving us glimpses of our own future, when we thought we were just stumbling through the present.

My advice to you is to spend some time reflecting on the things that God gave you to put your hand to early in your adulthood. They may be things that you attended to and walked away from, thinking that season was over, but what if that season was not about that season at all? What if it was a sort of training for you to do it all over again, perhaps on a different or more personal scale?

God, who exists outside of time, is remarkably aware of how precious time is to mortal man. In knowing so, He wastes none of our days. Our steps are ordered by Him, each to move us closer toward a specific goal. He's moving us that direction, often completely unbeknown to us.

FOUR

A Hint of Things to Come

—॰॰॰—

Our tenure at the boys' home meant an adventure every day. Kelsey was tasked with grocery shopping, which meant four or five carts of groceries at a time, all loaded into a fifteen-passenger van that she'd need to leave running outside the store, because -35 degree weather can cripple a vehicle in minutes if it's left sitting. Part of my role was to run the excess energy off the boys, so we'd range western North Dakota on fishing trips, sometimes using a small fishing boat that belonged to the sponsoring foundation. We learned to appreciate and love these boys. They were arrogant, rough, proud and wounded all at the same time. An issue would arise among them and it could end up in a raging fight, or two boys in tears, having come face to face with some of their own issues. It was gut-level ministry, and it was unconventional. It exhausted us, but we loved it.

During the season we were at the boy's home, we felt I should go ahead and pursue ministerial credentials with our denomination. I had never been a stellar student in college, so the idea of taking a test that would somehow qualify me for ministry was terrifying. The pastor of the local church served as a great encouragement, and loaned me his office to take the test as the denominational overseer waited. I'm not sure which one of us was more surprised when the test was graded and I'd done well.

Shortly after, we began asking ourselves if perhaps we should reconsider serving on a pastoral staff again. The boys' home had been a tremendous growth experience, and we believed we'd had a lot of positive influence on the boys the Lord had placed in our care, but we felt a stirring that we couldn't ignore.

After making a few phone calls to friends in ministry across the nation, we learned of a church in Kingsport, Tennessee, that was looking for a youth pastor. At that point, I knew one person in the state of Tennessee. John was a youth pastor in Memphis. I was so ignorant that I didn't even realize Memphis was as far as you could get from Kingsport, and still be in Tennessee, so I called him to get his perspective.

"John," I said, "I heard that a church in Kingsport is looking for a youth pastor."

"Yes, I know the church!" John replied.

I was excited—I'd found my connection! "Really? What can you tell me about them?"

"Well, I can tell you that they just called to offer me the job," he said.

I couldn't believe it. The only youth pastorate I'd heard of was calling the only common acquaintance we had to ask if he wanted the job. This is not how networking was supposed to work. Finally, I asked, "Are you going to take it?"

"No," he assured me. "I am very happy in my current role. Would you like me to call them and ask them to consider you?" Within minutes, John was calling the senior pastor and telling him to watch for my meager resume. We made phone contact in the following days, and eventually were invited to make the trip from North Dakota to Tennessee for a proper interview.

In an effort to save a few dollars, we flew to Cincinnati, Ohio, planning on driving the seven hours down to Tennessee. The trip got off to a strange start. We landed Saturday afternoon and discovered our luggage was not on the plane. Knowing we had to be in church—a church we knew almost nothing about—the next morning and would be evaluated as potential staff members, we drove directly to a mall. In 45 minutes, Kelsey bought a dress and I bought a suit that was at least a full size too big. Nevertheless we made it to Kingsport, dressed for church in the south, with a proper suit and tie.

That weekend was a blur, but in the weeks that followed we were invited to come and serve on the staff as associate pastors, leading the youth group as well as a number of other areas of responsibility. In retrospect, it seems my rapidly purchased suit and tie weren't quite proper enough for the congregation. On my first Sunday they presented me—on the platform, during the service – with a proper black preachers' suit that I was expected to wear every Sunday morning.

Proper Southern church attire was not the only lesson I had to learn. In our excitement to move as soon as possible, we had asked the pastor to find us housing for the meager budget of $200 per month. Initially, he tried to get out of it, suggesting, "Why don't you live with a family until you find the right place?"

After over a year of living with eight boys, we were ready to be on our own again, so I insisted, "No, you find a place, I'm sure it'll be fine."

Some things in life you look back on with a spirit of "If I knew then what I know now..." That decision is among those things for me. The pastor was a wonderful man, but I had no idea what I was getting into by asking him to locate housing for us.

He called me a few days later to tell me that he'd found us a place to live within our budget. Excitedly, I pressed for details. He didn't offer a lot except that it was a two bedroom trailer house not far from the church. I was hoping for an apartment, not a trailer, but quickly adjusted expectations.

"Is it in a trailer park?" I asked, trying to visualize what we were getting into.

"Kind of," He replied.

I began to get a little concerned. "When you say 'kind of,' what does that mean?" I pressed.

"It's not really a trailer park like you would think of it. But there are a collection of trailers there," he said.

I was confused and the only person with the information I needed wasn't helping things much. I prodded, "Well, it's not like it's in a gravel pit or something, is it?"

The silence on the other end of the line was deafening. "Funny you say that, Pastor Randy." He called me Pastor Randy the entire time we worked together. "It actually is right next to a gravel pit."

A few weeks later, with eyes wide and mouths agape, we drove up to our new home. We literally drove "up." The steep, gravel grade that we needed to climb to get there necessitated taking a hard run at it or one would lose all momentum and need to roll back down for a second attempt. At the top of the precipice was a 14' x 70' trailer, perched precariously on a pile of gravel so steep that the backside of the trailer, the part that held our bedroom, sat a full ten feet off the ground on railroad ties. In Colorado, grades this steep were marked Black Diamond. In Tennessee, they were plumbed for water and rented to youth pastors.

Just as promised—and feared—immediately to the south was a gravel pit. Its border ran right up to our little gravel driveway, and any trucks heading east from the pit would drive past our trailer and down a steep hill to the highway.

We tentatively unlocked the door to the trailer, hoping to find a diamond in the rough. We were not rewarded for our optimism. The interior of the trailer was filthy. The brown carpet, once shampooed, revealed itself to be burnt orange. A few days later, we met our landlord, a local fireman named Charlie, who had purchased the trailer on a whim. He looked around sheepishly and shook his head. "Kids..." he said. He called us "kids" every time we talked. "Kids, this is no place to live."

I didn't bother pointing out the irony that he actually owned this place that was unfit to live in and had rented it to us. He confessed, "Kids, I wouldn't want my own kids living here. I wish I wouldn't have rented it to you. I know you have a six month lease, but just as soon as you find something, you go ahead and rent it."

We did. A few months later, we bought a little 800 square foot house behind a gas station. It was humble, but it was home, and we didn't fear it sliding down the hill at night or being hit by gravel trucks during the day.

If the boys' home was our baptism into the unconventional, then Kingsport was our grad school in conventional ministry. At the time, the prevailing theory among large church staff leaders was to allow staff members to specialize. That theory did not prevail in this case. The senior pastor had a philosophy that an associate pastor should be able to do everything the senior pastor does.

While at times I wished I was able to concentrate more fully on specific initiatives, in retrospect, this was a huge blessing to me, as I was able to fill in all the holes that are inherent in a classroom education. It was not unusual for me to be called away from preparing for a youth group event to do a funeral, change a light bulb, or sit in on a difficult counseling session. As much as I'd have preferred to avoid them, I learned so much in those difficult duties.

In getting ready for one particularly dicey conversation with an angry parishioner, I noticed the pastor writing full sentences on a yellow legal pad. I asked him, "You're going to write a script for this conversation?"

"No, not really, but I promise you that at some point in the conversation, I'll say what is written on this page, and I'll say it the way I want to say it right now, when my head is clear and I'm not angry. And I won't say any more."

Although my title was that of associate pastor, there was great expectation that I would "grow the youth group." I discovered that my youth pastoring skills had not improved greatly since I decimated the small youth group I took when we first left Bible college. It wasn't the teens' fault—actually, I had the cream of the crop. They were great kids who genuinely loved Kelsey and I, but I was never able to build the bridge from that personal affinity for us into the action of inviting their friends or building our group.

I believe it's safe to say that if there was a book written about how to build a youth group, I read it in those years, and if there was a new theory thrown out at a conference, I tried it. Regardless, we never saw the corresponding growth happen. Our group would swing between forty and sixty teens each Wednesday night, whether I was preaching my heart out or playing games. I was giving it my best and still hadn't quite figured out that my best would never be good enough. It was the topic of more than one serious conversation between the pastor and me. He had served as a youth pastor at a much larger church and expected similar results now. Try as I might, the numbers didn't come.

Time passed quickly in Kingsport. We busied ourselves with the work of the ministry and started a family. Our eldest son, Jackson, was born there, and later a second son, Grayson, joined us.

The fifth year of our tenure there, God began to move on a congregation in Pensacola, Florida, under the leadership of Pastor John Kilpatrick and evangelist Steve Hill. Hundreds of people were giving their hearts to Jesus in extended services that were being held five nights a week. We heard reports of people standing in line all day to get a seat. I was about at my wit's end with the youth group, having given it my all for five years and my all clearly not being good enough.

My senior pastor was intrigued as well, although I'd eventually learn that he was approaching it from a different angle. It was a church within our denomination, which in those days, would have meant it was a safe one to explore. Even though they were "one of us," they were seeing things in the way of prophecy and healing that, while we would have given verbal ascent to, were beyond our experience.

After a number of months of talking about it, it was decided that our senior pastor and his wife would drive down to visit the meetings, along with Kelsey and me. The five years of laboring and feeling like I was missing the mark had taken their toll. We were treated wonderfully by our church, but I felt like a failure for not being able to make something happen.

I desperately wanted to hear from the Lord, and was naive enough to believe that others had the same motive. We found our way to seats along the left side wall and I determined to get all I could. I was so hungry for the affirmation of the Lord that it was all I could do to stay in my seat.

When the music started and the people jumped to their feet to worship, my pastor pulled out a yellow legal pad and started to take notes. He scribbled down all sorts of details—the types of songs that were sung, the way the stage was configured, and how the lights were set up. I didn't understand at the time, but he was evaluating the service as a production. As we debriefed on the way home, he told me, "You know, our music is as good as theirs. We do things well. I think we can see the same things in our church that they're seeing there."

In that moment, it dawned on me that I'd come looking for an encounter, while he'd come looking for a formula. Understand that by revival standards, I did not have the massive encounter experience that so many did. I had gone to the front at the end of the service to receive prayer.

One of their leaders had graciously prayed for me, but unlike so many around me, I didn't have the physical manifestation of shaking or falling to the ground. In fact, I felt that nothing had really happened at all, at least on the outside. Still, somehow, I knew what I'd seen there was more real than what I had been trying to do for those five years.

On that ride home though, hearing this revival reduced to where the piano was sitting or when they took the offering, there was a pain in my heart that reinforced what my head had begun to suspect: formulas were the work of frustrated men, and my heart was aching for the work of an all powerful God. I knew I wasn't dumb or lazy, and that if there was a secret to moving people's hearts I would have found it—but there wasn't. God had to be involved or we had nothing.

Back in Kingsport, my senior pastor was happy he'd made the pilgrimage, if only to affirm what he thought—that we had a great church. On the other hand, I made plans to return to Pensacola with my youth group. Even though I hadn't felt the touch I so longed for, I saw that people were receiving from God there, and I wanted my teens to feel it. That Thanksgiving, a convoy of vans and cars with forty-plus teens made the trek to Pensacola.

Our schedule allowed for two nights at the revival. The first night, our teens didn't know what to make of the music or the long services. The worship leader, Lindell Cooley, was an animated fellow with an incredible voice. He would pull from a wide catalog of music, playing everything from old spirituals to Wesleyan hymns, with an occasional Bob Dylan cover thrown in. Our teens didn't necessarily dislike it, but they weren't sure how to respond. When the meeting was over, we left for the hotel room, with me wondering if I'd wasted a lot of time and money bringing them down. Surely you couldn't affect change simply based on hunger, could you? Hunger seemed to be all I could muster. By the time the second meeting came, most of my teens had already mentally checked out. They were there, but they were also aware that we were leaving early in the morning, so in their minds, this was something to check off the list and head back home. From our seats in the balcony, they sang along with the worship, but more out of a desire to be polite than real expectation.

Early in the worship service, Kelsey excused herself for a moment to go get a drink of water. I sat by myself, afraid we'd made a massive mistake in spending the time and money to bring them all down. Maybe we did need a better formula, because this wasn't working either. It occurred to me that Kelsey had been gone a very long time. As I pondered what my next step was, one of the teens motioned for me to look over the balcony. Near the front right side of the stage, among a teeming crowd of worshipers, stood Kelsey, both hands raised, tears streaming down her face. I remember thinking, "I guess you didn't find the water fountain."

As I watched her, wondering what she was doing down there, her eyes opened and her face changed as if she saw something I didn't. Her body was thrown to the floor, as if by an unseen force, and she lay there stone still for a good fifteen minutes. Then she slowly started to get up and the entire scene repeated itself.

At the time, I was more than a little quizzical about all this, and forty minutes later, when she dragged herself up to our seats, I asked her what happened. She wasn't a lot of help. She could barely talk, and when I pressed her for an explanation, the best she could do was mutter, "It's the glory of God...it was like a wave. And I could sense it coming..."

As an analytical type, that wasn't cutting it for me. "What wave? How? Did you trip?"

She had no answers. Regardless, I knew my wife well enough to know she'd had some kind of encounter.

The service eventually finished and I sat watching my teenagers stand around waiting for my nod. They were finished and ready to head back to the hotel to sleep for a few hours. I was trying to mesh my wife's indescribable encounter with the boredom and apathy of the teens who had been in the same meeting. The longer I sat there, the more frustrated I grew. I was so sidetracked that I failed to notice that the room was emptying. Soon, it was only my forty teens, a few adult leaders, myself and a few people on stage.

Not wanting to miss anything God might have for us, I jumped up and followed the last guy leaving the stage—Richard Crisco, the church's youth pastor. He had his jacket on and was headed for the door when I caught him by the arm and said, "Pastor, you don't know me, but I'm a youth pastor from Tennessee, and honestly, I'm desperate. Would you pray for my teens?"

It was so late and they'd prayed for so many, I half expected him to say no, and wouldn't have thought poorly of him if he did. The lights were off in the sanctuary by this time. It was clearly time to go home, and these staff members did five meetings a week. Nevertheless, without a bit of frustration showing on his face, Reverend Crisco turned around and said, "Certainly." With that, he started to take off his jacket as he walked back toward the front of the stage.

I rushed back to our seats and gathered our teens down front. Many of them were frustrated with me because they were ready to go back to the hotel. I was extending this experience further than they were expecting it to go. Back at the hotel, we had Cokes and ESPN. Why was I dragging them up into this prayer line? Out of respect for me, though, they came and stood in line, patiently waiting.

If what happened to Kelsey earlier spun my head, what happened next blew my mind. With no drama or fanfare, Richard Crisco walked down the line of kids, touching each young person on the forehead and praying for perhaps ten seconds before moving to the next one. It was the most reserved and non-dramatic thing I'd seen at Brownsville. Standing ten feet away, I could barely hear him speak. The only way I could tell that God was up to something was that as he would move from one teen to the next, the one he finished praying for would drop to the floor like they were dead.

To clarify, they would not stagger back. They would not kneel. They simply dropped straight down as if every ounce of their strength had been zapped. Some flopped forward on their faces. Others fell back on their shoulders. Miraculously they didn't land on one another, because they were dropping like flies.

As he walked down the line quietly praying, he left a swath of bodies in his wake. The first few kids had no idea this was coming, but those at the other end of the line had a few minutes to watch and stood wide-eyed, wondering what was happening to their friends, and more importantly, if it would happen to them. As he drew nearer, some of them braced themselves. They wanted God, but they weren't going to be pushed. Richard didn't push. God did. Every student and sponsor found themselves on the carpet.

As he reached the end of the line, he collected his coat from the intern who was with him and quietly whispered, "Bless you," as he squeezed my arm and walked out the door, never looking back.

In seven minutes flat, Richard Crisco had wrecked my youth group. He left it and the sponsors lying on the carpet and me—their youth pastor—wondering what had happened.

I sat on the edge of the stage for a minute to gather my wits. Slowly, a few kids were starting to sit up. Many were weeping uncontrollably. Others were silent. A few still lay where they fell. As much as I wanted to run after Richard Crisco and scream, "What on earth was that?," I had the sense that this was a holy moment. I was afraid my tendency to process events and demand immediate answers could suck the life out of the experience for the teens. As quietly as we could, we loaded them into vans and drove back to the hotel. A few were still so incoherent that they needed help to get into their rooms.

I have little memory of the physical act of driving the six hundred miles back to Tennessee the next day, but I know what I was thinking about, or rather, what I was asking God. Over and over, I prayed, "God, what does this mean?" While I was hungry for a touch from the Lord like this, I didn't want a touch from Him that did not have a corresponding response from the kids. My deep fear was that we would visit the revival and nothing would happen. My even deeper fear was that we would visit the revival, something would happen, but we'd return home and stay the same.

As things would transpire, I had nothing to fear at all.

FIVE

A Study in Opposites

Once we returned to Kingsport, I wasn't sure how to relay what had happened to parents or church leaders. The first few days around the office, several people asked how the trip went. I'd shrug and reply, "It was great." Technically this was true, although it didn't encompass all of what happened. I simply didn't want to talk about something that I didn't have language for or experience in. I wasn't denying that it happened, but I wasn't going to position myself as the expert, either. I let the kids talk among themselves and tried to steer the conversation toward a "how then shall we live?" direction.

A few days later, we had our first youth service. We would meet in a gymnasium attached to the church, which meant I would spend about an hour setting up chairs and a sound system on Wednesday afternoons. As was my habit, I set the sound system up first so that I could listen to music while setting the rest of the room. Once it was all plugged in, I put a Lindell Cooley CD in the player and turned my attention to the rest of the job. As I pulled racks of chairs and tables from a storage room, Lindell's rich voice filled the gym.

Lord I groan, Lord I kneel
I'm cryin' out for something real
'Cause I know deep in my soul
There must be more.

My heart skipped a beat for a moment like it does when some-one finished your sentence for you...except in this case, it wasn't even a sentence I knew I was saying.

Lord I'm tired, yes I'm weak
I need Your power to work in me
But I can't let go, I keep hanging on
There must be more.

I stopped pulling the racks of chairs for a moment and stood straight up. Lindell's voice resonated through my body as the Holy Spirit identified the prayer of my heart. While I loved our church and our youth group, I was aching for something more than I could program or produce. I had worked so hard for years with little success in the natural—and I'd given it my best. I needed something more than my best to make up the lack in my own life and the lives of the kids I was leading. There must be more.

As the song continued, I felt a level of emotion well up inside of me that I would not have told you was even there five min-utes earlier. Nearly six years of doing it in my own strength had convinced me that "buckling down and working hard" might actually be a spiritual gift. In reality, I didn't know much about the Father's gifts. I was sincere, but most of what I knew involved my own efforts. I stood there in the corner of the gym and cried big crocodile tears that rolled down my cheeks and onto my starched white shirt.

I felt the love of the Father like I had not felt it in a long, long time. I heard Him thank me for my service, but assure me that He wanted to work differently with me now. I kept wiping my eyes with my shirtsleeve, but the tears just kept coming.

Finally, I recovered enough to get the tables and chairs set out. I went back to my office, regained my composure and put the finishing touches on my message for the youth group that night.

Like most every Wednesday night, we had teens show up an hour early to play basketball and horse around. I moved among them, laughing and talking, but never referring to my encounter that afternoon. I wasn't sure if I should say anything, or what I would say if I wanted to. The service started normally, with a few announcements before worship. Worship went well—a lot of the kids who'd been on the trip to Brownsville had taken their experience with God as a marker in their life and were very intentional about entering into worship. This was encouraging, but even then, it wasn't anything that was markedly different from many other Wednesday nights.

I have no idea what I preached about that night. I'm fairly confident that no one else would remember either. What I do remember was the high school football player who, despite the best concerted efforts of both myself and God, had completely ignored whatever was officially going on at the front of the room in favor of holding court with his buddy in the back row. I called for kids to gather and stand for prayer, he goofed off. We worship, he goofed off. I preached, he goofed off. At least he was consistent.

At the close of the message, I did what I had done for every other youth meeting over the years. I asked kids who needed prayer to come forward and invited others to pray for them. Some weeks this was an extended time of prayer, but often it seemed like a formality with little or no response. Based on my message and the general lack of interest, I assumed I was looking at the latter on this particular night.

Much to my surprise, the young man who had goofed off through the entire service stood up and walked down the center aisle between the two sections of chairs. My first thought was not that he was coming for prayer, but rather that he misunderstood, thought the meeting was over and was headed for the door behind me. Instead, he stopped right in front of me and quietly said, "I'd like someone to pray for me. I've gotta get right." When I recovered from my shock, I motioned for a few of my leaders to pray for the young guy, while I continued to direct the prayer time for the rest of the group. I stepped three steps to the left while two others gathered around him. As I said a few words to the others, they gently laid a hand on his shoulder and began to pray.

In seconds, this giant football player was sobbing. He wasn't crying silently, he was sobbing, chest heaving, shoulders shaking, snot hanging down sobbing. I was trying to maintain my dignity by fighting my curiousity, so I intentionally looked the other direction, until I heard him exclaim, "Oh God, Oh God, Oh God," in rapid succession. I looked his way just in time to see him fall backward and land flat on his back on the hardwood floor. The two volunteer leaders looked at each other for a moment as if to say, "Uh...now what?" We had no protocol for this sort of thing. We'd never needed it before.

Meanwhile, on the other side of the room, a slender sixteen-year-old girl I'd never seen before was having her own appointment with God. She, too, was crying but managed to stay perched in her chair. As others gathered around her, her story became known. She was the daughter of a drunken Baptist deacon, who was far from God herself. Her history was one of boyfriend after boyfriend as she looked for the love of a father. God was doing spiritual surgery on her heart, giving her all that she so desperately wanted. She was telling the kids praying with her, "I didn't even know this building was a church...I was driving by and heard a voice telling me to stop here, so I did."

To my right, the snot nosed football player was laid out like a cord of wood. To my left, the divinely invited party girl shook under the power of God as she confessed her sins. In the middle sat the same fifty kids who I had been ministering to—in some cases their entire junior high and high school years. Many of them were thinking the exact thing I was thinking. "What in God's name is happening?" Then, not quite sure what was going on but too desperate to miss it, many of them began to cry out to God on their own. They found private places of prayer in the corner of the room or huddled in groups. The service that normally finished at 8:15 p.m. stretched on until nearly 10 p.m., with adults who had come to pick up their teens left standing in the back because Little Johnny was stretched out on the floor praying for revival.

From that point on, our youth group made several sharp adjustments. I gutted our service schedule of anything except worship, preaching, and responding to God's word. I'd spent nearly six years trying to out-MTV an MTV generation and failed miserably. I'd discovered life in a simple presentation of Jesus and so that's what we did. Each week we saw kids come to Christ and be set free. Our little band of fifty that I could not manage to grow any larger quickly grew to a hundred. In many ways, it was more than I could ever have hoped for, yet the words of Lindell's song rang in my ears. There must be more.

Kelsey and I made a number of trips to Brownsville in those months. I didn't understand half of what I saw there—and honestly, I didn't like a lot of it—but I did know that they were operating in power that I had not tapped into, and talking about things that I had no experience of. Kelsey was quicker to receive new ideas from the Lord than I was, adopting some of the Brownsville language, such as describing things that were signposts from the Lord as prophetic. I actually told her, "Don't say that...no one agrees on what it means, so it's just confusing." Nevertheless, I knew there had to be more—more than my experience and more than my understanding. Even more than my expectation.

As the youth group experienced this time of God's power being poured out, and Kelsey and I moved further into this world of expecting God to do more, we found ourselves facing difficult questions from church leaders. They weren't openly critical, but neither were they tremendously supportive. They were concerned that the youth service went so long. They wondered if all this demonstrative worship was really glorifying God or just kids seeking attention. And what if the Wednesday night youth meeting eclipsed the adult meeting in appeal to the point that adults were trying to sneak in to the youth?

I had to admit, the services were getting long. We weren't worshiping any longer than we had before, and I wasn't preaching any longer than I had before, but the prayer time around the altar would go for an extended period of time. I wasn't sure that was a bad thing.

To be honest, the demonstrative worship was a little odd for me too. I was raised by non-dancers, the latest in a long line of non-dancers. We didn't dance at weddings, we didn't dance at parties, and we most certainly didn't dance at church, so to see these kids dance before the Lord was a little disconcerting to me. I was concerned. Maybe I was a little envious, too. Regardless, like the longer services, it didn't seem like a deal breaker to me.

As for adults trying to sneak into the youth service, I had to admit that it did concern me, but I was willing to post guards if necessary. I certainly didn't want to dull down our meeting to the point of equilibrium with the other meeting. I decided that the chance of a few adults sneaking in was worth the risk, and certainly better than going back to the way things were before we started encountering this season of the Lord's visitation.

Interestingly, at the exact time we were enjoying this period of passionate worship and interaction with God, we were deeply impacted by what some would have considered a nearly-opposite stream of influence.

We had gone to Cincinnati to spend a week of vacation with Kelsey's parents. It was rare that we were away from our church on a Sunday, so we got up Sunday morning not quite sure what to do with ourselves. We were too tired to really dive into action but too religious to go back to bed. Instead, we did what most people do on Sunday mornings—leave for services late. We were headed across town to another church of our denomination, realizing we were going to miss half the service because of our late start.

As we drove down a back road trying to make up lost time, we slowed for people walking across the road. I don't mean five people. I don't mean fifty. There were literally hundreds of people crossing left to right, and hundreds more crossing right to left. In the middle, directing traffic, was a guy wearing a jumbo neon plastic hand making the "number 1" sign like you'd find at a football game. Next to him was a guy with a combination backpack/drink dispenser, handing out cups of coffee to people walking either direction and to drivers of cars that were backed up as a result of the impromptu crosswalk. I asked Kelsey, "What on earth is going on?"

She spotted a familiar logo and said, "Oh—it's the Vineyard. I used to attend their services in high school once in a while. They met in a square dance barn back then."

"What kind of church meets in a square dance barn?" I thought. I guess the same kind of church that backs up traffic both ways and sends people out to appease the crowds with hot coffee. Curiosity rose up within me. "Do you want to go here instead?" I asked.

Kelsey agreed. We parked in a gravel parking lot and joined the throngs of people walking across the road. They were literally from all walks of life and more surprisingly, all stations in life. Young and old walked alongside the yuppie, the hippie and the homeless. If there was any common identifier among them it was that they were generally dressed casually—my khakies and dress shirt identified me as a newbie—and the fact that more of them than not carried a coffee cup. I began to wonder if I had found my lost tribe.

We made our way into the small foyer and found it crammed with people shoulder to shoulder. The building had seating for about 600, and although we didn't know it, weekend attendance for the Vineyard was about 3500 at the time. They managed this by adding services until they were doing eight every weekend, two on Saturday, six on Sunday. They had purchased the building from another congregation, who had felt they needed more space because they were unable to grow past 500 in such a facility.

We elbowed our way past the massive coffee dispensers and along the left wall, where we spotted a stainless steel rack full of bagged groceries. A sign on the front of the rack caught my eye. It read, "If you or your neighbor need a bag of groceries, take one!" Having personally operated in a real spirit of suspicion of other people for so long, I read the sign and blurted out to Kelsey, "Whoa – they are going to get ripped off big time."

Again, Kelsey is often quicker than I to see what the Lord is doing in a given situation. She had tears in her eyes, thinking of all the poeple who were being freed to do ministry on their own initiative. She looked at me and, as kindly as possible, asked, "What do you care?"

"Huh?" I replied. "This is an administrative nightmare! Who knows how many of those bags disappear every week!"

She repeated her question. "What do you care? What difference does it make to you? People are being trusted to do ministry on their own, and if they lose two or three bags of groceries a week in the pursuit of getting hungry people fed, don't you think it's probably worth it?"

I knew from the tone of her voice that she wasn't really expecting an answer. She was making a point. As much as I had grown in my understanding and appreciation for the work of the Holy Spirit in the months leading up to this, I still operated largely out of fear and suspicion toward other people. I wanted a move of the Spirit, but in regard to others, I wanted to be in control.

About this time, the service ended and people began to file out. We fought our way upstream and into the auditorium. It had a decidedly understated appearance, a simple stage, inviting lighting, and the distinct smell of coffee. It wasn't the sight or smell that captured my attention though, it was the sound.

Like most youth pastors who serve in the same community more than three or four years, we were often asked when we might want to pastor our own church. I had decided that I really didn't want any part of that, and so I'd invented a glib answer that usually shut the conversation down. I'd tell them that I'd be happy to pastor whenever I could find a church that would allow my favorite band to play an offertory. I said that confidently, knowing no church in the world that would allow this band to play—at least, no church that I knew of.

Ten seconds after we walked into the auditorium of the Vineyard, someone hit the play button on a CD player somewhere and that very band launched into my favorite song. It was a divine poke from the Lord and it caught me right in the ribs. My one defense against pastoring—even though it was a silly, made up excuse—was shattered in a moment. I glanced at Kelsey and asked, "Do you hear that?" She laughed—and cringed—because she knew what hearing that song meant. It meant my days of easy excuses were numbered.

Even so, neither of us fully comprehended how this church and its radical commitment to staying outward-focused would shake us every bit as hard as the move of the Spirit in Brownsville did. Without our perception, a tiny pebble had started to roll down a snowy slope. It would gather speed and mass until we were moving along with it, going where we had no intention of going, faster than we ever would have chosen to go there.

SIX

Divine Dreams

—ɷ—

Our first visit to the Vineyard left me shaking my head. We loved the church we were ministering in, even with its unique challenges and having to navigate an unanticipated outpouring of God's Spirit in our youth meetings. Even so, something about VCC resonated with me deeply. Kelsey chuckled at me all afternoon because that morning's service was all I could talk about. In fact, I was so fascinated with the place that I wanted to return to the evening service, almost to see if they could pull off something so unique twice in a row.

The Sunday evening service was the same as the morning service we'd attended. Because of the large number of attendees and the tight quarters, all eight services each weekend were identical. Nevertheless, I sat through the entire service with no less sense of amazement. This was church for people like me.

In the moment, I would have told you I was awed by its real-life approach to Christianity, its casual dress, its conversational tone, and its broad range of attendees. After six years of black suits every Sunday morning, this real-life approach to coming to meet with God was refreshing. In retrospect, it was more than that. The

Vineyard was one of the most permission-giving experiences I'd ever had.

Following the service, we milled around the foyer for a few minutes, as I picked up every piece of print material I could find. As we did, a smiling young man approached us and asked, "Hey, are you guys busy? We're going on an outreach and could use a few extra hands."

I glanced at him and said, "Oh, thanks, but we're new here." Obviously, outreach was for the trained experts. We might have been church-hopping felons for all he knew.

His smile never deteriorated, but his eyes crinkled up around the edges. He said, "Oh, I figured that. I saw you picking up brochures. You don't need to be a regular. You just need to have a pulse. Can you come with us? We're going to deliver some groceries to some hungry people."

We were expected elsewhere so we weren't able to go along, but as we drove out of the lot, his words rung in my ears. You don't need to be a regular. You simply need to have a pulse. Here was a place that was going to let me engage, at least at a rudimentary level, without the litmus test of commitment that is so often the rule in the church.

In striving for purity of doctrine and a high standard of conduct – both excellent goals—most churches place the bar one must clear to meet these standards too near the door. Very few people get their lives right with God and then come to church. Most come looking for God and carrying their baggage with them. They arrive on our doorstep broken, trailing broken marriages, addictions, estrangements with children, and wrong ideas about God Himself. Beyond the church stoop they hope to find the God of Fixes, but in trying to get to Him, they meet the Church of Qualifications, and they can't get past the entrance exam. The church, in trying to ensure the integrity of its membership, applies the rigors of belonging to those who are still trying to figure out who God is, let alone what He wants.

Acceptance and belonging are two markers of relational development that most of the church has backward. In more churches than I'd care to admit, one needs to cross the threshold of belonging before the hand of acceptance is extended. Until you belong—by membership, by leadership acknowledgment, or by public declaration—you are not offered acceptance. You are one of The Others.

On the surface level, the local bar has a better model. You're accepted as you are from the moment you walk through the door. That doesn't mean you're given the stage or preferential treatment, but neither are you on probation. You are who you are—boisterous, quiet, harsh or gentle—and people make their decisions about you based on your behavior. They may not like who you are. They may even avoid you, but it's not part of a trial. They simply feel no overwhelming pressure to reject you at first glance.

There is a teeter-totter that balances in every social structure. On one side is grace, on the other side, demands. As grace increases between people, demands decrease. Inversely, as demands increase, grace finds itself diminished. If you've done any marriage counseling, you understand. The young couple you meet within that pre-marital counseling appointment has nothing but grace for one another and almost no sense of demand. Call it naive, they really do believe the best about one another and are willing to love open-handedly. Regrettably, by the five year mark, some of them will have tipped the teeter-totter. Hearts will have been hurt, walls will have been built, and grace will have been pushed down as demands grow high. If they progress in this route toward divorce, by the time it nears finality, neither of them will have much grace for one another. I've heard of one spouse at the point of divorce railing against the other for the way they take out the trash.

Too often in the church, belonging is the predicate to acceptance. Newcomers are greeted, but often for the purposes of vetting. How many children do they have? Home-schooled, public or private? What's their church background? New believer, hardcore ideologue or theological mongrel? What are their values for worship, for giving, and for outreach? Upon discovering if they are one of us—if they belong—we then extend the hand of acceptance. Membership, official or otherwise, before acceptance is the rule.

The Vineyard turned that paradigm on its ear for me. It extended acceptance to those who came through the door, confident that the power of God could change their lives before they found their way into leadership or influence. The warm-hearted, "Come as you are," threw me off balance, or perhaps more properly threw me into balance with the Spirit.

That week, as we returned to Tennessee and found our way back into our routine, the young man's words and other concepts that I picked up from their printed material stayed at the forefront of my mind. I immediately dug into "Conspiracy of Kindness," written by their pastor, Steve Sjogren. It was part congregation history, part ministry philosophy, part outward-focused manifesto. Sjogren's words made me rethink so many things I'd taken for granted about evangelism and unbelievers.

Over the coming months, we remained in this double helix of influence, encountering the power of the Holy Spirit in our Wednesday night meetings and thinking about church in new ways that approached the community with open arms. We made frequent trips south to Brownsville to encounter the power of God and to observe how this move of God was stewarded. Likewise, every time we found ourselves in Cincinnati over the next year, we caught as many Vineyard services as we could. We couldn't get enough of these two radically different facets of God's hand.

As we remained faithful in the place we were planted, we quietly began to pray about what God had next for us. Perhaps some of our advisors were right and it was time to take a senior pastorate. On a whim, we sent a resume to a church we knew was looking for a pastor. For weeks we waited for some sort of acknowledgment—a yes, a no, or anything. We never got so much as a "Thanks for your resume." In retrospect, it seems that God doesn't respond to our whims.

At one point we interviewed with another senior pastor who was looking for a successor. He hoped to pastor for a few more years and hand off his church to a younger couple. There were a lot of positives in the situation—we liked the area and we liked that the church was debt-free. We also hit it off well with the senior pastor. He was warm and encouraging of the things that we felt called to. We walked out of the first meeting feeling that "maybe this is what God has for us..."

When you're looking to make a major move, you really hope for more than a maybe. This looked like a great opportunity and we both liked the pastor and his wife a lot. Still, we couldn't muster excitement about moving. We had all agreed to pray about it for a week, but a few days later, at home, Kelsey and I admitted to each other that while it felt good, it didn't feel right.

At the end of the seven days, I dreaded the call I knew would come. "Good morning, Randy!" an excited voice came over the phone. It was the pastor we'd interviewed with the week before.

"Good morning," I replied, hoping I sounded at least a little excited. I wasn't.

"We've been praying about you and Kelsey coming, and we really feel like it's the right thing to do. How quickly can you move? Let us know what you need and we'll make it happen."

"Pastor..." I stammered. "We've been praying a lot the last week..."

If ever disappointment was transmitted silently over the phone, this was the time. He waited for me to finish my sentence.

"Kelsey and I really enjoyed meeting you and your wife. The entire situation sounds amazing. We just don't think it's for us. I'm sorry. We're not going to take the role."

I don't remember much of the conversation after that. I'm sure we muttered our way through affirmations of one another, but it was pretty brief. With that, I hung up the phone without a clue what we were going to do next.

The pastor was so shocked by our response—our interview had really been an amazing time—that he called back ten minutes later. "Randy, I just have to ask you...from our perspective, our meeting seemed to go so well. Did we do or say something that offended you guys? Because I really felt that this was going to work."

"No, Pastor. You didn't do anything. We completely enjoyed getting to know you, but Kelsey and I really believe we've heard from the Lord. We don't think this is what is next for us."

With that, we closed an attractive door, not sure if or when another one would open or not. It is a difficult thing to say no to an opportunity that appeals to your heart and appears to please God's people at the same time. Had we gone to minister there, I'm confident the Lord would have used it...but I'm not confident we would be who we are today. The most difficult decisions we make in life are never between right and wrong. They're always between good and best. This was a good opportunity, but it was not best, and so we chose to wait for best even though it was nowhere in sight.

In the months to follow, I spent a lot of time in the church sanctuary in prayer. We loved where we were serving and felt the love of the people. Our relationships with the other leaders, our students and their parents were as fulfilling as ever. Still, we couldn't get away from the gnawing thought that there was a next step for us and that it held pieces of what we were encountering in the Spirit, and learning about how to accept people.

One Saturday morning, Kelsey and I were enjoying a lazy breakfast. Three-year-old Jackson played on the tile floor nearby and Grayson, our second son, was on the way. I'd had a thought on my mind for three or four days but hadn't been able to verbalize it to Kelsey yet. This thought threw out whatever bit of safety we knew as a family and frankly, it scared me as a husband and a father. Still, it weighed on me like a brick. As she refilled my plate with pancakes, I stared at the syrup bottle and blurted out, "I think we're supposed to plant a church."

Up until that point, if I'd been forced to make a list of things I never wanted to do, "plant a church" was certainly in the top five, ranked higher on the list than "ride a tiger" or "catch a bullet." Somewhere in my Bible college days, a strange idea had planted in my head that church planters were guys who were unable to find a conventional pastorate. Since then, my thinking has shifted to believe that the only people who take conventional pastorates are those who can't plant churches, but the moment I said "plant a church," it certainly didn't sound appealing.

I shifted my eyes from the syrup to my wife, expecting things to be no less sticky there. This was the farthest thing from our minds. We'd never even talked about it in jest, and here I was suggesting it in all seriousness. Kelsey swallowed hard, turned on her heels and walked out of the kitchen.

"That didn't go too well," I thought. In our seven years of marriage, she'd never walked out of the room like that. Fortunately, she returned in a few moments holding her journal. She opened it to a specific day, pressed it down flat on the table in front of her and spun it around so I could see it. Then she pointed to the last sentence on the page and flatly said, "Read this."

There, in my wife's handwriting, I read, "I think we should plant a church...but I'm afraid to tell Randy." It seems the Lord had spoken the very same thing to her in prayer a few days earlier, and she was struggling with how to tell me because she feared I'd flatly reject it.

I can't describe the joy that came over us. It was as if we were both looking for the way out of a dark cave, stumbled upon the entrance from different sides, and shouted to one another in unison, "I found it! Over here! Over here!" We didn't know how long the entrance was or when we'd see daylight, but we did know we'd made significant progress and could feel the fresh air blowing on our faces. Now we had more than drive. We had direction.

My first order of business was to admit I didn't have a clue about church planting. I started reading every book I could get my hands on. This may have been my single biggest mistake, but it did give me something to do in the waiting season, because even though we knew we were to plant a church, we didn't know where.

Our first foray into discerning a location involved calling our denominational district headquarters. The state leader was very excited about the idea—he'd come to know us a little bit over the years and was happy we were looking to go about it "the hard way." I believe he meant this as encouragement, but it failed miserably. A few days after our initial phone call, he called me again and asked, "What do you think about Franklin, Tennessee?"

Immediately my interest was piqued. Franklin was the booming southern fringe of Nashville. It featured a funky downtown square and a reputation for fast growth. All the books I read told me this would be a good idea.

"We own a church building about three blocks off the square. Would you and Kelsey consider taking it and planting a church there?"

We were interested...and we were going to be in Nashville in a few weeks, so we decided to do a drive by. We loved the town square. It was easy to imagine a bustling church of young people tucked into this trendy part of town. We circled the square in concentric circles until we found the building. We had assumed that the church had been long closed, but were surprised to find that it was still in operation, although obviously struggling.

I called the denominational leader and asked "Is that church still open?"

He took a while to answer, but finally said, "Yes, it is...but not really. That pastor is going nowhere. We need to move him on and get some life in there." Then I realized that we weren't being called in to plant a church—we were being asked to kill one.

I thanked him for thinking of us but stressed that we wanted to plant a church and that this was probably not the right opportunity. I didn't follow the situation, but knowing how things work, I'm sure they found an assassin somewhere. I was just determined it wasn't going to be me.

It was becoming clear that there was no instant way forward. We were being impregnated with God's idea of the church that we would plant. To take over an existing church and reshape it into what we were called to build sounded dishonest, disingenuous, and frankly, more work than starting from ground zero. In the short term, it might be easier to have a congregation and a building, but we knew that the values we were trying to embrace—radical pursuit of Christ and a radical spirit of generosity and openness—would challenge an established congregation.

Reminded of the old adage, "It's easier to give birth than to raise the dead," we set out to give birth to that which God had placed within us.

SEVEN

Location, Location, Location

—ɷ—

Driving in East Tennessee was vastly different from driving up in my native North Dakota. On the North Dakota plains, roads ran east and west or north and south. All intersections were 90 degree corners. If you could imagine a checkerboard in your head, you could maintain a mental map in North Dakota and navigate far from home.

In East Tennessee, roads twisted back and forth like spaghetti spilled on God's earth. Our church receptionist insisted that thirty miles from us, across the mountain in North Carolina, there was a road that passed the same tree three times. I laughed at her—until I had to drive over for a funeral and discovered she was right.

Driving in Tennessee was a good primer for planting a church. We had turned a major corner—decided to plant rather than take an established church—only to discover there was another corner looming in front of us. Once we decided on what to do, we were faced with the bevy of questions that followed, not the least of which were "where" and "how."

We loved the area we had lived in for nearly seven years. East Tennessee had been good to us. We'd married young and begun to grow up there. We'd had two sons born since we moved there.

We loved the people of our church, the terrain of the mountains that lie to the north, east and south, and the easygoing nature of the community where it was impossible to go to the grocery store without seeing people who you knew and loved. The question of "where" to plant a church had to be asked in relation to where we were. You don't move without clear direction.

Tentatively, I approached my senior pastor to discuss the idea of our current church helping plant locally. The idea caught him off guard, as we'd never discussed it before and he felt strongly called to build a large church in our current location. A church planting project would require finances and people, but he was open to talking about it. Over the course of a few weeks, we spent several hours driving around the community, scouting locations, and talking about what it might look like to partner together. On what would be the last of these exploratory drives, the real source of his concern surfaced.

Driving down a twisty East Tennessee lane, he said, "I believe we could do this...even commit some finances to it and allow you to continue to serve on our staff in the transition, but I would need some assurances."

I had been very pleasantly surprised at his willingness to discuss it. Given the opportunity, we would much prefer to not have to move—at least out of the general area. "What sort of assurances?" I asked.

He struggled for words, but finally said, "I would need assurances that you wouldn't build your church too close to mine."

What he was saying didn't register fully for a few minutes. In my mind, what we were hoping to do was so radically different from our current church that it was difficult to imagine anyone leaving the mother church to attend the church plant. Granted, some people probably would have, but most of them who enjoyed their own church wouldn't like what we felt the Lord was asking us to do. The vision was that different.

"When you say too close," I asked, trying to press for specifics, "How close is too close?"

He pulled the car into a small shopping plaza parking lot and pointed at a sign. "Beyond that sign," he said.

"Huh?" I replied.

"If you plant a church in East Tennesse, it has to be on the other side of that sign. No closer." We were about fifteen miles from the home church. "If you build it on the other side, I will help as I can. You can't build it on this side."

I sat for a moment, soaking in all that this meant. It was awkwardly quiet in the car. He turned the car around from what was apparently the edge of the Church DMZ and headed back to the office. We didn't talk much as we drove. He seemed sheepish about having drawn a line. I was a little embarrassed too. I wasn't shocked that he was afraid of us being too close, but I was pretty surprised that it came down to the specific location of a county sign. I was hoping for a Paul and Timothy encounter and instead felt like I'd been given an Abraham and Lot moment.

As we pulled into our church parking lot, I broke the silence. "Pastor, I don't think we're going to plant it here."

"Really?" he asked, trying to mask his relief.

"Really. You and I know that if you have to draw a line in the road and can only bless it on the right side of a specific geographical marker, then you're really not excited about this. You're enduring it. And I don't want to ask you to endure something. We will go."

There were two dynamics at work here. On one hand, it was our first experience bumping up against a territorial spirit. I don't use that phrase in the sense of the demonic—this was a good man doing what he felt called to do, and the idea of another local church pastored by a well-liked pastor from his congregation seemed to threaten that. On the other hand, the Lord used it to expand our thinking until we found the exact spot where God wanted us. As disappointed as we were with what felt like the left foot of fellowship at the time, it wasn't long before we began to see that the

Lord was leading us, and even this experience was part of it. It also wasn't much longer until we saw that this territorial spirit was far more common than we realized.

Having decided that we would need to move to follow God's call, we spent hours talking, praying, and staring at the pages of an atlas (this was before the days of Google earth!). I'd always wanted to move west but couldn't in good conscience pretend that it was the call of God. We didn't think we wanted to go east. Further south didn't seem right either. More often than not, we would get up and walk away from the table leaving the atlas open to southwestern Ohio.

Kelsey had grown up in Cincinnati. Kelsey's parents and brother still lived there. We loved visiting several times a year. It was the city where so many of our presumptions about ministry had been blown apart by Steve Sjogren and the Vineyard. Could it be that we were being called to plant a church there?

At the time, we were part of a denomination that dictated where new churches were started. They would have shunned the term "denomination," preferring the more genteel "cooperative fellowship," but as one of my college professors had noted, "If there is no cooperation, there is no fellowship..."

I called the denomination's headquarters in Ohio and asked who I might talk with about starting a church there. In moments, I was forwarded to the office of a nice man with a warm voice, who was elated that we might consider coming to Ohio to plant a church. After getting acquainted I explained to him that we would be in Ohio in a few weeks. We made plans to meet for breakfast and talk about what God was calling us to do.

Years have dulled a few of the details, but I'm pretty certain the meeting took place in the corner of a Bob Evans. I'm certain there were pancakes involved—and syrup as well. I'm also sure that things got sticky quickly in more ways than one. We took fifteen minutes to tell our story and explain how we were led to think about planting. He took fifteen minutes to tell us his story and how he ended up directing church planting. Then he put down his fork and asked, "Where are you thinking of putting the church?"

Kelsey and I looked at one another, smiled, and answered nearly in unison: "Cincinnati."

For a moment, I thought he'd gotten into some rancid syrup. He unsuccessfully tried to hide a quick facial contortion, picked up his fork again, and studied his sausage patty like it was an object that had come back from the moon. Finally, he managed a response. "Why Cincinnati?"

Looking back on that meeting, I'm pretty sure it was the first "why" question he'd asked in a meeting that was full of why opportunities. We had told him we were leaving a successful church that we loved. He didn't ask why. We told him we were diving into starting a church with nothing. He didn't ask why. We told him God had called us. He didn't ask why. We gave him a large geographical area of where we wanted to place the church and suddenly, he became very interested in process. I was becoming acquainted with Church Planting Theorem 1.1: everyone is in favor of church planting somewhere else.

We gave him the rough answer—that we felt the Lord had highlighted Cincinnati, that there seemed to be life in our hearts when we talked about it, we had family there and it was home to a church that had influenced us greatly.

"Have you considered Lorraine?" he asked. To be truthful, we hadn't. I wasn't even sure if Lorraine was a place or a person, but I was positive she'd never come up in the conversation.

"Not at all," I replied. "Why?"

"We need a good church in Lorraine. Now. And in Buckhead Lake. And Sandusky, and Wilmington. Have you considered any of those?"

I admitted I had never considered any of those places. If he'd asked, I would have also admitted that I didn't know any of those places existed. In my confusion, he pressed in.

"Promise me something. Promise me you'll consider those places. Pray about it. Go to them. Walk the streets. See what the Lord is saying."

Now, fifteen years older, I would respond differently. I would say, "I have heard what the Lord is saying. He's saying go to Cincinnati." Instead, I just replied, "Uh, ok."

Kelsey and I were pretty discouraged when we walked to the car. We knew that we were supposed to plant a church in Cincinnati. That bit of divine information was probably the clearest direction we'd ever gotten from the Lord. Yet over a breakfast with someone who didn't know our name a few days earlier, I'd committed to considering at least five other locations that I now needed to go find on a map. We were fatigued at the thought of a setback and even more distressed that perhaps we'd not heard God as clearly as we thought.

A few weeks later, we took some time off from our church in Tennessee to return to Ohio to honor the promise we'd made. Basing out of a friend's house, we charted a course that criss-crossed the state, putting us in each of these cities over the course of five days. As we drove, I tried to encourage myself. Perhaps this is a good thing. The Lord moves in mysterious ways. Maybe we will love these cities. Maybe we missed it. Just a side note—when your attempts at self-encouragement include "maybe we missed it," you're slipping into self-delusion.

Our first target was Buckeye Lake. We'd been told that it was a booming little community just east of Columbus. We headed there with great expectation. A town on a lake sounded quaint – and it was—but absolutely nothing about it resonated with us. Hoping for fireworks that might signify this was God, we couldn't even find a snap, crackle, or pop.

Next on the list was Lorraine, situated on Lake Erie, just west of Cleveland. Approaching it from the south, we passed through Oberlin, home to the famous Oberlin College and the place where Charles Finney was buried. We took this as a good sign—Finney had embodied the kind of fiery passion for God that we hoped to have. Driving into Lorraine, all warm fuzzies for Oberlin and Finney's grave simply fizzled. We drove up and down the streets looking for some sort of sign from God, and found none.

Eventually we found ourselves pulling into a little parking lot overlooking Lake Erie's cold waters. We were tired and discouraged. Nothing about being there felt right or appealing. Standing there in the park that bordered the lake, we felt the wind that whipped across the water, and for just a moment I thought I could hear Gordon Lightfoot's "Wreck of the Edmund Fitzgerald." Later I learned that the ship named the Edmund Fitzgerald actually sunk in Lake Superior, not Lake Erie, but I was pretty certain that the idea of us planting in Lorraine would suffer a similar fate.

Checking Lorraine off our list, we got back in the car and headed west, keeping the lake to our right and all of Ohio to our left. We spent the night in Sandusky and the next morning, felt the same way we did about Lorraine and Buckeye Lake before that. By the end of the day, we'd traveled 500 miles, never left the state of Ohio, and were convinced we'd not seen any place we were being called to plant a church in. Understand, this is really no reflection on these communities. I'm sure they all needed churches. We simply couldn't muster the enthusiasm for a place other than where we had placed our hearts. We weren't rejecting other locations—we were unable to turn our back on what we'd said yes to originally.

A week later, I called the denominational office and was patched through to the church planting director again. "So," he asked, "What did you think? Did you like Buckeye Lake?"

"No." I thought about offering caveats, but I had none.

"Lorraine?" he queried.

Again, I replied, "No." I went on. "And it's not Sandusky, either. We looked at all five places, and I'm certain that none of these are where we're supposed to move to start a church."

"How can you be certain?" he asked. "You've only thought about it a few days!" I found this strange, because had we answered in the affirmative, it was quite obvious that he would have done handsprings across his office and helped us with moving expenses. It seems one is able to decide to move across the country in only a few days and that would be celebrated, but deciding not to puts one under great suspicion.

"We've thought about Cincinnati for months." I countered. "We want to plant a church in Cincinnati."

On that decision, the discussion took a turn. He grew very quiet and said, "If that's the case, then I suggest setting up a meeting with the local leaders, to see if you can get their blessings. And frankly, I don't think they'll be open to it."

Local leaders had never been mentioned in our discussion of the other cities, but that didn't strike me odd at that time. What I did find unusual was after offering to pave the way for us in several places, when we rerouted back to Cincinnati, we were on our own. The message was clear—you can plant in Cincinnati, but you won't get much help from us. In the end that turned out to be inaccurate. The denomination did help financially and we were grateful—but it only came after we were clear that we were going to plant in Cincinnati, with or without their help.

I made a few phone calls to known leaders in Cincinnati and was steered toward the area church planting committee. The chairman was a pastor who'd labored in the Montgomery area of Cincinnati for many years. When I told him what we hoped to do, he invited me to meet with himself and two committee members. After my interaction with the state leader, I was prepared to face the gauntlet. Instead, Kelsey and I were warmly greeted and seated at a table with three other men. "Tell us your story," they said.

By this time, we were learning that telling our story was a large part of planting. After sharing who we were and what we felt God was calling us to, we stopped and asked if they had any questions. "Just one," the chairman said. "What do you want?"

I wasn't sure I understood the question, so I asked him, "What do you mean?"

"From us," he replied. "What do you want from us?"

At that moment, it occurred to me that I'd never really considered what I wanted from them. Perhaps it was that I wanted them to tell me we weren't crazy. I stammered for a second and then said, "Your blessing. I want your blessing and I'd like to plant this church as part of your fellowship, but know that we will plant this church." In answering him I found a resolve that I didn't know God had been forming. I was committed to do this, with or without the approval of men.

The chairman closed his portfolio and leaned back. For a moment, I thought I'd overplayed my hand. Then he smiled and replied, "Well if that's it, I don't even know if we need to vote! You're just the kind of people we want moving to Cincinnati to plant a church. Let's do it. You have our blessing. And we'll try and do more than that."

We were ushered out as quickly as we came in. Once out in the foyer, the youngest member of the committee came out after us. "Randy, Kelsey!" he called. We stood in the foyer and he explained that he represented a church in the city that had long wanted to plant in the very area we were wanting to target. "We have held off because we didn't have the right couple. I think you're the couple. Would you consider partnering with us?"

Thirty minutes later, we drove back to Kelsey's parents' house in stunned silence. We'd gone from feeling like we were fending for ourselves to having the support of locals and a specific church that wanted to take us under their wing. Could things get any better? If ever there was a situation set up for success, this was it!

If only we knew what was to come.

EIGHT

Launch Mode

—m—

We moved to Cincinnati in the spring of 1999. After the initial week or two of setting up our household, we put our hands to the work of starting a church, which greatly accentuated a problem that I'd been worrying about.

I had a strong sense of calling, but I didn't have a strategy. For the previous seven years, my role as a staff pastor had been tightly structured. The list of mandated to-do's was fairly long, leaving little room for creativity. I am not exaggerating—my eight page job description included a bullet point that said "lock doors when leaving." That is not a joke. At least not intentionally. When you don't use a muscle, it atrophies quickly, and living for seven years with my creative arm in a cast left it a little puny. It took me awhile to remember that it was okay to dream and that there was no one to stop me if I wanted to act on those dreams.

That summer, our host church gave us the run of the place, connecting us with small groups and asking me to teach a class on Wednesday nights. Through these opportunities and other contacts from Kelsey growing up in Cincinnati, we connected with several couples who were interested in planting a church and seemed convinced that we knew what to do.

We had rented an apartment in a complex in the Kings Mills area, in part because its large clubhouse would be available to us for meetings. In the late summer we booked the clubhouse for a Vision Night to share the story and vision of the church we felt called to lead.

The day of the meeting, our host pastor had arranged a morning coffee appointment with Steve Sjogren, pastor of the large Vineyard that had been so influential in our decision to plant. We had been going to our host church Sunday mornings, but had been attending the Vineyard Saturday nights to learn more about how they did things. I was captivated by Steve, who I always felt was communicating on multiple levels. I'd met him briefly in the basement of the Vineyard where I chased him down to ask him to pray for me, but we'd never really had a substantive conversation.

I'll admit to being a little nervous. Okay, a lot nervous. Steve was an enigma. Bigger than life, he'd based his ministry on the radical idea that the kindness of God leads people to repentance. In the previous year, he had a terrible medical accident that meant an extended hospital stay and rehabilitation time. I remember him making his way with a cane to our table in a local coffee shop, and positioning himself gently in a chair.

Excited about our plans for that evening's meeting, I launched into our story of how we were church planting and that we were about to have what we hoped would be a wildly successful recruiting opportunity. Even as I spoke—too quickly and too much, I'm afraid—Steve looked at the floor. At first I thought he was tired. Then I worried he was bored. It would be months later, as I got to know him, that I realized he had an uncanny ability to take in information even when he appeared to be in another world.

As I explained that we were about to meet with a group and make a pitch for them to join our efforts, he finally broke his silence. "I hope you gain a lot of traction. And a lot of people sign on. But don't get too attached. They'll leave in two years."

I stared at him for a moment, thinking I'd heard him wrong. Surely this wasn't meant to be encouraging. I couldn't even look at Kelsey. When I was able to formulate a response, it was something along the lines of, "Huh?" Finally, he continued, "The people you will gather tonight...God will bring them. And in about two years they'll leave. And that's okay. You need scaffolding to build a building. Some people are scaffolding, they're only there as it gets started, then they leave. But they're useful and it's really God. But if you think they're there forever, you're going to be really disappointed."

With that, he muttered, "I need more coffee." He stood up and shuffled over to the coffee bar with his cane.

As someone who had idealistic notions about church planting, this was not the sort of coaching I expected. In my perfect world, people teamed together for a lifetime, building community and never detaching. It bears noting that this idea existed entirely in my head. I'd never actually done it, nor seen it done and now, a hero of mine sat before me and burst my bubble. To this day I don't know that Sjogren's theory is true 100 percent of the time, but I will concede that he's more right than wrong.

Our meeting ran about two hours. After having the expectations for that night's meeting deflated, I found myself hanging on Steve's every word. He didn't talk or think like any pastor I'd met. He had an undeniable charisma, but beyond that, an intuitive way of thinking that led him to make broad, authoritative statements, which I'd question at first and later come to agree with. I didn't know if we'd ever connect again, but I hoped we would. I certainly didn't expect to develop a friendship with him that would guide much of my thinking about ministry.

That evening, we gathered twenty people or so to cast vision for a new church. I was shocked at the quality level of people who God was sending. Some were raised in the church and looking for a fresh expression of Christianity, while others were very new believers — like our next door neighbors. They brought skills to the table – in business, in technology, and in ministry. I had heard Steve talk earlier that day about how many dysfunctional people church plants attract, but apparently word hadn't gotten around to them, because to me the crowd looked like the church planter's dream team.

After coffee and snacks, they all settled into overstuffed chairs and couches that sat around the club house, and I took my place in front of the fireplace to share what we felt the Lord was leading us to do in church planting.

That night's meeting went by in a blur. It felt as if I started with, "Good evening and welcome..." and was hitting, "Let's pray..." about thirty seconds later. I was as nervous as I'd been at the birth of our first child. The idea of asking people to commit substantial amounts of time and money to an unproven idea—that we could plant a church—was horrifying to me. It wasn't that I didn't believe in the idea, but rather that I feared no one would go with us. In trying hard to win their support, I made my first obvious mistake of church planting. I made it too easy.

Rather than talk about the hard work of planting, I talked mostly about reaping. I could see them getting excited about being part of something where a lot of people were coming to know the Lord. I couldn't imagine that they would want to be challenged upfront with the amount of work it would take, and so I minimized the cost and maximized the benefits of a church they could think of as their own. This misstep early on would plague me for the duration of our time there. It was not that they were not willing to work, but rather that I did not lay out the opportunities well or develop leaders from within the core. Ever since, in leading other teams, I've sought to compensate for those first mistakes by challenging team members with the question, "What do you want to be doing a year from now that you're not doing now?" and trying to help develop their skills to the point that they grow spiritually and in their leadership skills.

My error in minimizing the effort needed and not developing leaders within was not entirely my fault. At the time, I really thought it was easier than it was. I had read several books that gave me a real one, two, three approach and I was smart enough to follow directions. Additionally, I had met several successful church planters who, upon close inspection, did not appear to be the sharpest knives in the drawer, yet they were successful, so I had a bit of a "if they can, I can" attitude.   The bulk of my mistake, however, lay rooted in the ridiculous notion that Sunday morning was the most important part of church life. I saw that most successful church plants had dynamic Sunday mornings, and I knew a dynamic Sunday morning had three elements: the worship, the preaching, and the over-all vibe.

We had brought a worship leader with us from Tennessee, so we had that third covered. I knew I could preach—seven years of holding high school and junior high kids' attention every Wednesday night gave me a confidence in that arena. The vibe, or intangible element, I was figuring out from my visits to the Vineyard. I just knew that if I could get this little band of followers to a Sunday morning context, this thing would explode.

Years later, the idea that a superior Sunday experience is all that it takes to plant a church seems laughably naive, but as the expression goes, you don't know what you don't know, and I didn't know how wrong I was. I'd learn that fast, but later.

I wasn't sure if I'd communicated well or not. It's hard to speak of the callings of your heart to a group of strangers, let alone ask them to buy in. Something must have worked, because over the next few weeks, nearly every couple at that meeting contacted me and indicated they'd like to be part of what God was going to do through this church plant.

What began as a meeting about a church plant became a series of Bible studies in our basement. In my early thirties, I was the oldest member of the group most of the time, with the exception of my own mom. She had moved to Cincinnati to live with us and quickly became the designated church grandma. Our fledgling congregation was mostly young, mostly married, and starting families. Those early months of evening meetings in our basement became memorialized as "The Basement Days" in our church lore. Given the difficulty with climate control, child control, and aversion to small groups, I am convinced that we remember them as more glorious than they were, but there was certainly a measure of joy inherent in those gatherings.

I cannot say enough good things about the people God sent us in those days. Years later, there is not a one who I would not drop everything and race across town to see if given the opportunity (we all moved and scattered across the country in the years that followed). We had great fun and connected with God, often in spite of my lack of leadership skills.

My first earth-shaker as a church planter was small groups. No one had told me how important leading small groups would be to church planting. I know that sounds crazy, but it never came up. I had preached for years, but the skill of preaching and the skill of leading small groups have almost zero in common, and when you're church planting, you start with a small group and are glad to have it.

Our weekly meetings were pure and simple—a little worship, a little teaching, and we'd pray together. The worship was good – nothing sounds better than twenty or thirty voices crammed in a basement. The teaching was iffy—I had a tendency to speak at people rather than with them, but people kept coming back so it seemed to be adequate. The prayer was hard.

Our congregation (it all seemed so organic that we would giggle if we were to refer to ourselves as a congregation, but in retrospect, I guess that is what we were) was made up of two sorts of people. The first part were young or new Christians who had never been taught to pray. They had no experience in talking with God and so at times it was stifled. They just didn't know what to say.

The second part of our congregation were established believers who had been raised in the church. Interestingly, they had little
experience in praying either—at least publicly—and didn't have
much of a better idea of what to say than the newbies. Yours truly,
the pastor, was squarely in that camp.

My impression of those early meetings was that the worship
was glorious, the teaching okay, and the prayer was awkward. Ending on an awkward note every week—waiting for someone else to
pray, desperately afraid they wouldn't, then discovering that they
would start the exact moment someone else did—was excruciat-
ing, because I felt that last impression was the one we all carried
all week. I would go into the next week's meeting in fear of that
awkward ending, even to the point of missing the good parts.

Our plan was to wait for what all the church planting gurus
called "Critical Mass"—that moment when you were bursting at
the seams and you needed to go to a Sunday morning format.
The reasons for waiting are too numerous to count. Everything
gets harder in a Sunday morning format. Expectations are higher.
Childcare for strangers. Signage. Rent. Some churches spend two
years in incubation, small groups multiplying like rabbits, and
launch with a thousand people.

I think we spent six or eight weeks and launched with
thirty-five.

In retrospect, I would have done things differently. I would
have forced myself to become a better small group leader. I would
have pressed harder and more specifically for commitments to
certain roles. I would have handed off more of the responsibility
and let others carry the load. What is life, though, if not a series
of experiences which, given the chance, you would do differently?

That fall, SpiritLife went public. We started with the intention
of a series of six monthly Sunday evening services.

As difficult as it is for a new church to find a place to meet, it's
even harder to find a place to allow you to meet once a month for

six months and then transition into a weekly gig, so our options were limited.

Our first service was held in the local high school band room. We had hoped to use the school theater, but the band was set up for a big concert. The band instructor was a believer who felt badly that he was setting our plans on edge, so he offered the band room. I quickly agreed.

I remember walking past the theater with its great lighting and seats, into the band room. I had never been in the room before it was time to set up for our first service. I was stunned. It looked like a band room. I'm not sure what I expected. Music stands were everywhere. There was a row of tubas hanging on the wall. I closed my eyes and tried to figure out how I was supposed to communicate the life-changing power of the gospel with tubas hanging on the wall. These are the things church planters think about—and often the reason they crash and burn.

What I don't remember is much about the service, except that we discovered that in order to properly greet people, care for kids, provide coffee, usher, etc., it took about forty people to produce a Sunday service. We had fewer than that, which meant we had some people doing two jobs. Everyone was working hard to produce an event that none of us were able to enjoy because we were too busy producing the event.

If I had known that this would be a picture of the next three years, I would have bludgeoned myself to death with a tuba.

The ironic part was that by the next Sunday evening service a month later, the theater was available, so we eagerly chose to upgrade for ambiance sake. Our numbers had grown a little and we reconfigured our volunteers. This meant that we actually had about thirty people in the seats during worship (the month before, if the band took to the stage, the seats were empty and we were down a nursery worker). Did I mention that the theater sat about 400 people?

Two months into our Sunday monthlies, I was jazzed. I was excited because finally I was able to do what I knew I could do—stand in front of people and communicate. It never occurred to me that the only thing that had really changed was the format. We didn't have markedly more people. The worship was not suddenly improved. We were just doing a lot more work to reach one or two more families than we were able to in my basement. I was oblivious because for the first time since starting to church plant, I was doing what was comfortable for me.

Looking back, this should have been taken as a marker of death, but I didn't realize at that point what an enemy comfort was to the kingdom.

NINE

Brother Bohlender

—◊—

There's nothing I like more on a cold, rainy day than a bowl of thick soup. It's comforting. And as food goes, it's idiot proof. If you have the ingredients and proportions right, you put it all in a pot and crank up the heat. In time, you're going to have good soup.

Church planting is not like making soup, because we had the ingredients. And we certainly had the heat.

Northeast Cincinnati was ripe for church planting. It was growing exponentially, primarily populated with well-employed young couples. You couldn't roll a bowling ball without knocking over a soccer mom or denting a minivan.

We were blessed with the best young couples any church planter has ever worked with. I assembled a board of young men who, along with their wives, became dear friends and responded in a Christlike manner to any instruction or request put before them.

I recruited our most important help even before moving from Tennessee. Melody had grown up in our youth group and had recently gotten engaged to Adam, a young guy from another church. They'd started attending our church and leading worship on Wednesday nights for youth. One night after youth, I made a ham-fisted pitch: "Come help us plant a church!"

After a little thought, they agreed that this was what God was calling them to. Their eager yes to that appeal remains one of God's dearest kindnesses to my heart. Only heaven can repay them for the hours of service they gave and encouragement they brought to the process. Melody worked tirelessly in any area she was needed. Adam's technical skill grew to match his creative genius. They helped us form the framework of what this church would be through countless late night talks and pots of black coffee.

In the coming months, we developed a set of values that I would go to the mat for even a decade later. Heaven knows we had to wrestle for them before we even started. Our denomination sent us to a church planters' boot camp in Michigan. We gathered at a campground with twenty other church planting couples from across the Midwest, and spent three days training and working through exercises that would help us determine our values.

On our list of values were two items that directly reflected two of our largest influences—the revival that had been going on in Pensacola, Florida, and the Vineyard in Cincinnati. Because of all that those two places meant to us, we included expressive worship and a user-friendly atmosphere on our list of values. We wanted it to be a place where people freely worshiped God—demonstratively if they desired—and yet anyone could walk in and figure out what was going on because of our intentional language and approach.

One of the coaches that weekend had been a key leader at Willow Creek, a megachurch in Chicago. He gave some of the most useful talks, but during the exercise of nailing our core values, we went head to head. As he looked at our list of five or six things, he pointed out those two—expressive worship and a user-friendly atmosphere—and said, "You can't do both. Pick one."

With that didactic pronouncement, he walked away. We shrugged and ignored him.

Later, he came back to the table where Kelsey and I were working. "Which of those two values are you going with?" he asked.

"Both of them," I replied.

"You can't. They counteract one another."

I disagreed, "No, true expressions of worship, properly explained, are not offensive to most people. Hype is offensive. Fake is offensive. If we are proactive about explaining our terms and behavior, people will accept it if it's sincere."

"I think you're wrong," he said.

"I know we're not," I said.

He smiled. "Okay. I just wanted to make sure you were willing to fight for it." With that, he walked away. The values stayed as written. Little did I know that I would be fighting for those values—and others—for the next three years, but not with consultants or congregants.

If we had any struggle other than our own failings, it was with our denominational representatives. I want to point out they were good people in themselves and bode us no ill will. Our difficulties were inherent in trying to do something new or different within a large, old organization.

Rare is the organization that does not calcify as it ages. The result makes it hard to be entrepreneurial in an established setting, because everything you choose to do seems like a threat to the establishment, whether it was meant to or not. I found this to be true from the very outset.

In preparing to move to Ohio, we prayed about a church name. We knew what we wanted to convey—the idea that life in the Spirit knew no bounds. We wanted to build a church that taught people things on Sunday morning that they lived and used on Tuesday afternoon. We wanted to erase the erroneous conceptions of church life and normal life. We eventually settled on the name SpiritLife, using no space between the two words to signify the unity of the idea.

On my paperwork for the denomination, I wrote SpiritLife. In my emails to the leaders, I wrote SpiritLife. During my phone calls, I said "SpiritLife." On my first quarterly review, about the time our small group started to meet, I gathered with several denominational leaders from a district office. They smiled through my brief presentation and followed up with a statement, not a question.

"Let's talk about what you're going to name the church," the ringleader said.

I was confused. "We already named the church. It's SpiritLife."

They smiled and nodded. Over the years, I learned that smiling and nodding was what they did before they told you no. "We understand that you have used that as a sort of working title, but now that you're becoming official, we had another name in mind."

With that, they announced their choice of a church name. It was two parts. The first part was the name of the suburb. The second part was the name of the denomination.

Keep in mind, I had no beef with the denomination. I was a product of the denomination. At the same time, branding this new congregation with a term that meant little to any of them and nothing to the community sounded like a bad idea from the get go. I pressed back, "I want to stick with SpiritLife."

They smiled and nodded, "We understand. But if this is going to be part of our fellowship, the name should reflect it. Otherwise, how will people looking for one of our churches find you?"

The phrase "one of our churches" made me slightly ill. "I hear you," I said. ("I hear you" was my equivalent of their smiling nod). "However, I am not primarily interested in people moving from one of the fellowship's churches to another. I am looking to build a church for people who have no clue who you are and wouldn't care if they did."

More nods. Fewer smiles. An exceedingly long silence. I'd go so far as to say an awkward silence. Finally, one of them spoke. "Brother Bohlender," he began. I knew things had shifted. I had been "Randy" a few moments ago. We were well on our way to "Reverend" or "The formerly Reverend..." at this pace.

"Brother Bohlender. We feel quite strongly about this name. But we are open. Perhaps you should spend some time in prayer and see what the Spirit says."

I agreed. In fact, I didn't just agree, I immediately bowed my head and prayed out loud. After my best audible two minute prayer that God would show us what the name of the church should be, I said, "Amen." When I looked up, the three startled faces across the table indicated to me that they had meant that I should go home, pray about it, and renegotiate with them by phone. To be fair, I had already prayed about the name for a significant amount of time, so I made an announcement.

"I think the Lord would have us continue with the name of SpiritLife. Thanks for allowing me time to take it before Him one more time."

The meeting was over and I was back out in my car before I realized that I had inadvertently done an end run around one of the oldest stall tactics in ecclesiastical circles—the nebulous "Let's pray about it."

Our relationship with the denomination continued in the same odd manner. It was never hostile. It was never tepid. It was simply one misunderstanding or missed expectation after another. I probably started it by saying, "I'd like to plant a church with the denomination," leading them to believe I wanted to start a church like the denomination. I wanted the fellowship, not the form. They couldn't conceive of fellowship outside the form. To further compound the issue, I became known for filling out the monthly forms with robot-like precision, putting them in the quandary of being frustrated with me for nebulous things while holding my forms up at church planting meetings to say "This is how we want you to do it."

The denominational tradition was rather formal. You will recall that in my previous post at a church of the same denomination, I was presented with a black suit on my first Sunday and told that I was expected to wear it. It was one of those things that you're glad happens to you in your early twenties because you don't know any better. If it happened to me now, I'd probably crack up laughing.

Our church, however, was decidedly informal. I wore jeans and sandals. We took a break between worship and preaching to grab bagels and coffee. Our young adult crowd sat near the front and often on pillows on the floor. We didn't have heavy church furniture—we had folding chairs and candles.

Understand, we weren't making a statement against anything. Instead, we were being practical. When you set up and tear down your church every weekend because you're in a borrowed or rented facility, you learn quickly that lighter is better.

About six months into weekly services, the secretary of a high ranking denominational official called me.

"Brother Bohlender," she said.

I didn't recognize her voice, but the "Brother Bohlender" was a tip-off regarding where the call was coming from. She continued, "Brother Bohlender, our district leader would like to attend your service in two weeks and install you as pastor."

My first thought was, "Install me? Like a dishwasher?" My mind raced a hundred miles an hour. My congregation of young people would have even less of a grid for a pastoral installation than I did. I knew the older minister and sincerely appreciated him, but I was trying to figure out what this strange meeting might look and feel like to both him and my own crowd.

"Uhm..." I stammered. "Our schedule is quite full, especially on short notice. Can we put this off for a while?"

"A week?" she asked. I was actually thinking months.

"Can I call you back?" I replied. She agreed, and I hung up the phone, feeling like I'd dodged a bullet.

Six months later I ran out of excuses, and he did come for an installation service of sorts. It was, as I expected, painfully strange for all parties concerned. He and his wife were very kind, but I could tell they wondered what they had wandered into. Likewise, my congregation was universally puzzled as to the nature of the service. I was their pastor because they'd decided to join the church, not because an unknown individual arrived to "install" me. Nevertheless, there were no casualties and the deed was done.

Months later, he asked a mutual friend, "Have you been there? They have...pillows. And a lot of candles." Our form was so far from his norm that it rattled him to think about it.

Over all, my bumps in the road with my denomination were almost entirely along the lines of culture and style. I was reading widely and drawing from a variety of leadership and thinking sources. Additionally, my budding friendship with Sjogren was leading me to realize that I may have spent the past seven or eight years in a well-constructed box. I was peeking over the edge of the box, wondering what was out there. In doing so, I no doubt made a few assumptions about the box itself—how small it felt to me and what I thought it might have been constructed of. In most situations though, it was a matter of two groups not understanding one another.

My only justified frustration with the denomination came from their tendency to offer extensive advice that often didn't fit my situation, while rarely asking me the questions that would be crucial to knowing what I was facing. I was subject to a lot of input—albeit little of it actually binding—but never really felt understood or even known. Most meetings and phone calls were decidedly one way.

I can recall at least a half dozen meetings that I walked out of shaking my head, thinking "Do they even know me?" One, in particular, brought the whole issue to the surface. About a year after getting started, a new contact person was assigned to me from the denomination. A former pastor turned denominational official, he was to be a coach of sorts. He called and asked if he could drive the ninety miles to Cincinnati and have lunch with me. I'd heard great things about him and was eager to meet.

At the time, the church had found a semi-permanent home in a small store front. It was the funkiest of arrangements—one long, narrow room with a glass wall on one side. Because the bathroom was in the back, it gave us no choice but to set up the room in a wide arrangement. We had fifty seats, but the third row was the back row. It was so bad that I was secretly relieved when people didn't come to visit.

We agreed to meet at the church for a bit so he could see our setup, then go to grab a bite to eat. What I am about to relay is going to sound as if I'm exaggerating, but I assure you, I'm not. It played out this way. In retrospect, I can understand how. He was young for his role and new in it. He was certainly well-qualified, but sometimes when you feel like you're in over your head, you have a tendency to overcompensate with words.

From the moment he entered our building and we shared introductions, he began to talk. He told me his history. He told me his vision. He told me his experience, his philosophy, his successes, and how he hoped I would proceed. He told me how he was selected for his role with the denomination. He told me a few stories about his most recent pastorate and how fulfilled he was in his new role.

Then he shifted into the advisor role. He told me how he might tweak the setup of the building. He told me what sort of outreaches might work in our community. He told me which pastors I needed to know and why. He was moving on to matters of church function and referenced doing weddings, when he did something he probably regretted later that day.

He asked me a question.

Keep in mind we'd been sitting together for well over ninety minutes. The idea of going to lunch had been lost in the flurry of input from him. In ninety minutes, he had yet to ask me a single question. With every minute of his unsolicited input being piled on, I grew more and more frustrated by a coach who was too busy coaching to even ask about the player's previous experience.

In referencing doing weddings, he asked a side question, almost rhetorically. "Have you done weddings and funerals before?"

"Stop," I replied.

He looked at me curiously. "Stop what?"

I cleared my throat, which had grown tight from an hour and a half of not being used. "Stop firehosing me with input, when you don't even know if I have the sense to do a wedding or a funeral."

Silence. Big-eyed stares. He was not prepared for a church planter who would speak, let alone challenge him. I took advantage of it and pressed in.

In a quiet, even tone, I said, "You've been here an hour and a half. In that time you've barely let me get a word in edgewise. Now it's clear that you're coaching someone who you know zero about. You don't know if I've done weddings, funerals, preaching, baptisms...you don't know my story. It is obvious you have valuable input to give me, but I'm not sure you can give it accurately without knowing our story."

That seemed to make sense to him, so I continued.

"Here's what we're going to do. I'm going to tell you our story. When we're done, you're going to know who we are and you'll be able to give me even better input with the perspective of where we've been and what we're about. I'm going to tell you that story front to back, and you're going to listen to me, or you can get in your car and go back to your office. What would you like to do?"

He blinked rapidly and muttered, "I, uh...would like to hear your story."

With that, I sat back and told our story. It was the longest version I've ever told. It was so slow it was nearly in real time. I told him about growing up in North Dakota. I told him about going to college, about meeting Kelsey, about our first ministry role in a small church in Kansas. I talked for another ten minutes at the church, then for the ten minute drive, and then for an hour over Mexican food. I told him every random fact I could think of about us, because I knew that more input was inevitable and I wanted to ensure that he had a grid to give it.

When I was running out of information and he was running out of time, I closed up my monologue.

"...And that's what you need to know about us. I am confident I can learn a lot from you—but you have to understand where we came from so you can point us where to go from here."

With that, he got in his car and left. Other than official emails with requests to fill out forms, I believe it was the last time we talked.

Again, overall, my experience with the denomination was not that they were bad. Contrarily, they were godly people operating in the system that God had used them to build over decades. They may have been a bit overbearing at times, but they were and are saints of God who are being used in a powerful way. It was more a matter of our not fitting, than them trying to force something.

A year later, Kelsey and I were on a double date with Steve and Janie Sjogren. Steve was asking me how my relationship with the denomination was going, and I relayed this story and others. With the afternoon sun shining down on him, Steve tilted his head back a few degrees and closed his eyes. I had come to recognize this habit and knew that he was about to drop a wisdom bomb on me.

"Whatever group you're part of, I think that it's important to be a light version of that group."

Like most Stevisms, I didn't understand immediately.

He opened his eyes, recognized my blank stare, closed his eyes and continued. "You need to identify and term who you are and let the greater group influence but not define that. You are certainly a product of your denomination, but you are also a product of other influences. Your church should reflect that—and that will always prove itself to be a bit of a sticking point to the larger group. I've always been a Vineyard guy, but our church has always been light Vineyard. That has probably frustrated some people, but it's provided the community a more accurate reflection of who we are. It's great to belong to a group, but don't go too heavy on it, because the community doesn't care what group you're part of. When it becomes most of what you're about, they don't care about what you're most about."

That comment gave me permission I didn't know I was searching for. It probably also charted the course for a decision I'd make later. Par for the course, Steve had no idea of the power of his own words.

TEN

Dreams and Wrecking Balls

—ɯ—

There are a host of qualities that a church planter needs to be successful. They should be comfortable speaking to others. They should be able to envision people. They should be good fund-raisers, organizers, and counselors. The most necessary quality of anyone pioneering any sort of work, however, is not skill-based. It can't be taught. It can be developed, but only through resistance.

The most necessary quality of a church planter is endurance.

When planting a church, you're asking people to help you carve a spot out of granite while simultaneously inviting them into that spot. It's tiring, frustrating work. More often than not, the guy who succeeds after years of trying is not the most talented guy who has tried it—he's the guy who just wouldn't quit.

One of the things that wore me down the fastest was our nearly constant state of homelessness as a church body. Ten years later, I can quickly think of ten places that we met in the two years of church planting. We were never more than a few weeks from being told we couldn't meet in our current location anymore, and I don't ever remember there being a season where I wasn't looking for a church building.

I realized how consumed I was with this when one day, driving through an urban section of the city, we passed an old, abandoned cathedral with the windows boarded up and graffiti sprayed all over the walls. My oldest son, then eight years old, looked out the window and observed, "Huh. They don't meet there. They must have found a better location." In his mind, that's what churches did. They moved.

We tried a variety of hotels in the area. Churches meeting in hotels quickly get ready for the Sunday Morning Surprise—it's when you arrive at the facility and discover what new and exciting thing is happening in the hotel and will somehow affect your service.

Perhaps there is a soccer tournament, and the hallway outside your meeting room is the registration area. In between worship songs you hear, "Ten year olds, sign up here! Don't kick that ball!" Other times, the hotel forgets to give you an important piece of information, such as, "Your meeting room flooded two days ago and the carpet is still soaked." Still other times, you arrive to find the room perfectly set—and smelling strongly of bacon. Some churches have great, long-term relationships with hotels. That was never our situation.

We shared a facility owned by a deaf congregation for a while. They met Sunday mornings, we met Sunday nights. I learned a lot about the deaf culture in that season. For one thing, their sense of humor is often very pointed. The pastor, who was deaf but read lips well enough to communicate well, had decorated his office with the mounted head of a mule deer. On the deer's head he had placed a set of huge, industrial quality headphones, because in his words, "The deer's the only one not deaf around here and he repeats everything he hears."

Perhaps we should have seen this coming, but the deaf church had little use for sound equipment or acoustics. They did use a tall, upright piano on which the worship leader pounded out chords with great enthusiasm. Few in the congregation were aware that the piano itself was so out of tune, that most of the songs were unrecognizable.

For our purposes, the biggest difficulty with using the facility owned by the deaf church was the horrible echo. It was not only strong, it was greatly delayed. Anything sung or spoken on a microphone would slap off the back wall and return to where it was spoken nearly a full second later. It was literally possible to sing a duet with yourself, in harmony. It was nearly impossible to preach. Fortunately for us, our crowd was so small that I often would forgo the microphone and just raise my voice.

At one point, I thought we'd found the perfect building. Near our home was a massive, 100,000 square foot office space that sat empty. I heard through the grapevine that there was a business theater in the building, and after several phone calls, was able to gain access to the property for a walk through.

Guided by the property manager, Kelsey and I walked past what seemed like miles of empty offices, each of them clean as a whistle. We were both thinking the same thing—this place would be perfect! There was room for classes, children, offices, everything we wanted to do. There was still a question about the auditorium – would it work for our needs?

The property manager guided us to a gleaming stainless steel elevator door. We looked at each other for a moment and tried not to smile. What kind of church goes from meeting in a bacon-smelling hotel room to a corporate setting with its own elevator?

Getting off on the second floor, he motioned, "This is the lobby to the auditorium." The lobby itself was twice as nice as any space we'd ever met in. I chortled.

Opening a door, he said, "Let me find the lights," and stepped into the darkness. I stood in the doorway, peering in. When the lights came up, I nearly fainted. Here was a 400 seat auditorium, steeply raked floor, hardwood stage, professional lights and a three projector system in the ceiling that would throw images on the stage backdrop that doubled as a movie screen.

I walked down the aisle and onto the stage. I could see it happening here. I could see the auditorium full, the band rocking, images on the screen behind me. This was the break we needed. Then I asked the question every planter delays until the last moment.

"How much?" I inquired.

"I don't know," he replied frankly. "We have never thought about renting it out."

"Well, if I needed a few classrooms and this room...can you find out what it would cost me?"

He nodded. "Our board meets on Monday. We'll talk then."

I pressed, "In the meantime—can we meet here on Sunday?" I desperately wanted my young families to get a look at this place and feel the potential—especially if it was going to cost us. He agreed, and we made arrangements to get a key.

That Sunday, we gathered and wondered. God, might You have something like this for us? Could it be our wandering days are over for a while? The meeting was amazing. Great acoustics. A beautiful facility. The preaching wasn't half bad either. I left the service like I hadn't left one in a long while—energized.

Early Monday morning, I had to catch a flight. That afternoon, on a layover in the Detroit airport, I couldn't wait any longer. I called the property manager to ask him what they'd decided to charge us for our new building.

"Oh, yes, hello Reverend Bohlender," he said.

Historically, when people pull the reverend card on me, it's not good news. This was no different.

He continued, "Thank you for your interest in the building. However, in the board meeting this morning, the board decided that rather than rent the property to someone, we're going to tear it down."

I nearly dropped the phone. "Uh, I'm sorry...you're what?" I couldn't imagine that what I'd heard was real. It had occurred to me that they may not want to rent it—but tear it down? "You saw the identical property next door, no doubt. It's another 100,000 square feet, and when the two buildings are full, we don't have enough parking. So we are razing the building." I saw my perfect building slipping from between my fingers. I wondered how much time we had left—surely this would take months or even years to arrange. "When?" I asked. "When will you tear it down?"

"Very soon," he assured me. True to his word, within a week, I drove by to see a wrecking ball smashing into the plate glass. Within ten days, the entire facility was level with the ground. They were painting the stripes for the parking inside of a month.

While it is true that we were inordinately discouraged because of buildings, a building was also used to stir faith and mature us in God. Near our home was a stately building on a well-groomed 40 acres. Formerly the home of the College Football Hall of Fame, it had sat empty for a number of years. It featured plenty of parking, 40,000 square feet under a roof, and its own 10,000 seat football stadium where the annual College Football Hall of Fame game had been held. We drove by the building several times a day and began to wonder, "Why not, God? Why should it sit empty while our church remained homeless?"

The building was owned by a wealthy family in town—the sort that everyone claims to know because it makes them seem important, but no one knows well enough to land a meeting for you. The family was well-known for their faith and philanthropy. We were full of faith and needed a philanthropist. This seemed like a match made in heaven.

Initially unable to make contact with the family, we began to pray that God would open a door for us to discuss it with them. We prayed at home, but with the building being so close to our house, we found ourselves pulling into the parking lot once or twice a week to pray from our car. That led to getting out and wandering the grounds. We would walk up the massive steps to stand on the huge porch-like front of the building. Peering in the windows, we could see that the building was in disrepair.

Sheets of wallpaper hung from the walls. Ceiling panels were knocked askew. Nevertheless, we felt as if we were falling in love with this building. In retrospect, we were actually falling in love with an idea.

About the time we began praying for the building, we started dreaming, day and night. We had no office space at the time, so most of my sermon prep was done at a bagel shop a few miles from home. I would sit at a window table with my Bible propped open, and it was as if the Scripture was a soundtrack for what was going on outside the window. I would read of God's power and in my mind, I would see it played out in our community. Kelsey was having similar stirrings, speaking often of a radical idea of night and day prayer. And it wasn't just us.

One day I received a phone call from a church member. She was young in the Lord, and we had been instrumental in discipling her. She wanted to speak to Kelsey and I that night if possible. We set a time and she came over to the house. I wasn't quite sure what to expect—Sjogren's admonition about people leaving always hung in the back of my mind. I was relieved to learn she wasn't leaving, but she was being stretched.

She began with a characteristically blunt statement, "I think I have ESP."

We replied with characteristic insight, "Huh?"

"I must have ESP or something. Because I feel things. Deeply. And I dream the same things. I'm sure they're going to happen and I don't know why I know."

Kelsey and I exchanged glances. I stifled a smile. "You don't have ESP," I told our guest. "The Lord is speaking to you. You have a prophetic spirit—you are sensitive and you're picking up on what God is doing. So what are you sensing?"

She wasn't sure she wanted to tell us. "It's crazy. It will never happen."

We pressed her, "You're not responsible for making it happen. Tell us what you're feeling."

"You know the brick building on the corner by the highway?" she asked.

"The Hall of Fame building?" we replied, suddenly very interested.

"Yes. When I drive by, I feel something. And I see it in my dreams at night. It is full of young people."

She started getting fidgety. This was real to her. To hear her tell it, this wasn't a dream—it was about to happen. She continued, "I'm directing traffic because they're coming by the bus load. They're coming because of the worship. The sound is drawing them and they're coming night and day."

Kelsey and I were both stunned. Our friend was hearing from the Lord the very things we were talking about and praying for. As weeks went by, we pressed in further in prayer and seemed to hear more. The Lord was speaking—but what did He mean?

It started to give us confidence to dream for more. As I would pray and drive by the building, my heart exploded with vision for the property and the immediate area. I was asking for a massive kitchen that we could prepare food to take to the homeless who lived downtown. I was asking for funds to buy the small houses that bordered the property on the south side, so that we could house single moms. In the deepest recesses of my heart, I saw the football stadium full of worshipers in day-long prayer and worship events.

Summer turned to fall and we were still dreaming. Somehow we procured the name of the property manager who worked for the family. In spite of his protests about the building being in great disrepair, we begged for an opportunity to walk through it. After weeks of trying to land a time, he agreed to meet us. We felt like the Israelites about to go spy out the promised land.

Pulling into the parking lot behind the building, we met the well-dressed man in his sixties. He'd spent his life working for the owners and was a trusted advisor. We shook hands and he began the tour with a list of disclaimers.

"The owners aren't really looking to do anything with the building. And whoever did buy it would need to spend a fortune. The heat might work, the A/C doesn't. And I think a lot of pipes are busted."

With that, he rolled open an overhead door on a loading dock and we peered into the darkness. When our eyes adjusted, it was like seeing heaven, if heaven turns out to be a huge, vacant building in disrepair. Dust hung thick in the air as we stepped through the door into a massive warehouse style area. I later described the size to our board as "big enough to drive a car in at forty miles an hour." I wondered if we weren't looking at what would become the SpiritLife auditorium one day.

Picking our way through boxes and over shelving that had been knocked over when the previous tenants moved out, we made our way to the finished portion of the building. We knew what was in the very front of the building, but other than those few rooms visible through the windows, we had no idea what lay within those walls.

What we found was remarkable. In addition to the massive room I saw as an auditorium, we found a dozen small meeting rooms surrounded by a grand central foyer. A teak paneled board room. An ice cream shop with an exit to a patio overlooking the 10,000 seat football stadium. And behind the ice cream shop (which I'd quickly dubbed the coffee shop), a 150 seat theater.

The potential was dizzying. I could see us meeting in the theater until we outgrew it, then moving into the rest of the building. It was a mess, but in my mind, we could meet there immediately. The owner's representative was more reserved.

"What is the potential for us to rent it?" I asked.

"It's a hard property to rent," he replied. "It needs so much work..."

"What if I fix it?" I said confidently. I didn't want to tell him that my lack of handyman skills was legendary. This was no time for that.

"I don't even know that it's possible," he said.

"I think it is," I replied.

He sighed, "Well, draw up a proposal and I will forward it to the owner."

With that sliver of hope, I smiled. We shook hands and parted ways. Over lunch with friends, our dreams grew bigger and our faith was stirred. What might God be wanting to do in that building? Years later we would learn the better question might be, "What might God want to be doing on the earth?"

In the weeks to follow, I researched the repairs and began to formulate a proposal that wouldn't believe the fact that I didn't know much about what I was asking. We also ratcheted up our prayers. Jackson, our oldest son, was learning to read. He would write Scriptures on Post-It notes and tuck them in the cracks of the walls. Grayson, our second son, would put his little four-year-old hands in his mother's and pray along with her.

Never in a million years would I have expected things to play out as they were about to. To be very truthful, I'm glad I didn't know then what I know now. Sometimes ignorance of the future is what keeps you believing.

In reality, the immediate future held more heartache than hope.

One of the reasons we were especially excited to move to Cincinnati was that Kelsey's parents lived there. They lived a very different life than we did but we loved them both dearly. Her father, Rick, was a sweet, cantankerous man who reminded me of Archie Bunker. Her mother, Roni, was a hardworking woman who would do anything for her grandchildren or her daschunds!

About the time we were getting ready to move to Cincinnati, Kelsey's parents' marriage fell apart. Years of heartache boiled over and Roni moved out of their home to move in with another man. Rick, who had been hard to live with for years, watched what little structure he had in life fall apart. He packed his bags one day and moved out of the family home, allowing it to go into foreclosure.

He soon moved in with a girlfriend. It all happened so quickly that our heads spun.

We received a lot of bad, ungodly advice from Christian friends in that season. In their desire to help us feel better, they would tell us, "You need to release them to get a divorce." We were hurt and confused, but we were pretty sure divorce was not God's plan.

One day, Rick called Kelsey from the Veteran's Hospital. He had been stricken with a rare cancer and was not doing well. We raced to the hospital to find his girlfriend in the hallway, where she told us in tears that this was not what she'd signed up for. The message was clear. In addition to being very sick, Rick was homeless. We invited him to move into our home when he left the hospital.

The next few months were bittersweet as Rick's health deteriorated while his spirit soared. He began to get to know his grandsons. He returned to the Lord. And his heart began to stir for his wife. He would call her at work to talk. Eventually he asked her to dinner. Kelsey and I, knowing he was absolutely broke, gave him twenty dollars to take her out.

"Kelsey," I said. "How weird is our life that we just gave your dad twenty bucks to take your mom out to dinner behind her boyfriend's back?"

Slowly, they began to warm toward one another. Before a full reconciliation could happen, however, Rick's body succumbed to the cancer. A few months after moving into our home, we raced him to the hospital where he lingered for a few days before dying.

Late in his illness, Roni had been seeing a doctor as well. Oddly, she too had contracted a rare cancer. The weekend that we buried Rick, we put Roni in the hospital for surgery. Knowing she would be weak, we moved her into our home when she was released from the hospital, thinking she would recover. Instead, she got weaker. Oddly, she also got stronger in the spirit. She had been led to the Lord by a co-worker a few months earlier. In her feeble condition, she wanted to be baptized. It was one of the greatest honors of my life to carry her small frame in and out of the baptismal. She could barely muster a smile, but she was experiencing new life.

Day after day, we watched Kelsey's mother wither in a hospital bed in our living room. We would take turns sitting up late with her as she would get confused and scared. I remember climbing into bed late one night to hear my wife quietly crying. She had lost her father and now her mother was dying as well. I told her, "Kelsey, if this doesn't kill us, we're going to be tough as nails." To be honest, I wasn't sure at that point which way it would go.

About one hundred days after losing Rick, I walked in to the living room and saw that Roni was not breathing. She had apparently died a few minutes earlier. The Christian station that we kept playing on the radio was broadcasting Steven Curtis Chapman's "I'm Free." Truly, for the first time, she was.

A few days later, we buried Roni next to Rick. They were husband and wife, at one with Christ, and in glory forever. I told Kelsey I felt like we'd helped win the race, even if we'd pushed the car across the finish line on flat tires and an empty tank of gas.

Even more than ever before, we felt we were pouring everything we had into Cincinnati in order to see His kingdom come.

ELEVEN

Believing for a Place

—◊—

One of the struggles of church planting is finances. We moved to Cincinnati with no guarantees—there was no one to guarantee anything! We had much work to do and weren't sure how we were going to do it. We were blessed and honored when the denomination offered us a small salary for the first year. It wasn't quite enough to make ends meet, but it was certainly more than we anticipated.

Of course, there are more expenses to planting a church than the pastor's needs. Things like office supplies, audio equipment, printing materials—all these were for us to figure out. This meant regular fundraising trips to missions conventions to ask other congregations to contribute. I actually liked this part of the job—I was much more comfortable speaking to larger crowds than I was to the small congregation that we'd assembled. Sometimes speaking big vision to a small number of people made the vision seem all the more ridiculous. It was one such trip that would set us on a nine month journey of wondering what God was up to next.

Our entire family—much smaller then, with just the two older boys—drove to Memphis for a missions convention. Scheduled much like the others we'd done, this event started with an evening banquet, with five or six of us sharing for a few moments. Then it allowed us to fan out across the city to preach in churches on Sunday. That Sunday evening I was in a lively congregation on the edge of town.

Our plans for the Hall of Fame building were so far out there that we normally didn't talk much about them. When you're visiting a church of 100 people, to tell them that you have your sights set on a multimillion dollar property doesn't help bring clarity to your need. For some reason, however, that night I spoke at length about what we felt God wanted to do on that property. I even inserted a few slides with photos of the stately building and football field. To be honest, I don't remember any specific reaction at the time. I remember more about eating McDonald's with the pastor's family after the service than I do about the service itself.

The one thing I do remember, though, is the middle-aged man in jeans and a work shirt who approached me immediately after the meeting. He was unremarkable in most every way—not the sort to stick out in a crowd.

He said, "I liked your story about that building. I'd like to help you. I'm a business man."

We shook hands and he gave me his business card. It was dog eared, as if it had been carried in his wallet for a long time. I remember thinking, "He doesn't hand out a lot of business cards." I also remember that the card gave no indication of what sort of business he was in. It listed his name, address and phone number.

"Call me this week, I think I can help you," he said before shuffling off. I stuck the card in my pocket and thanked him.

The next morning we pointed our van north and headed back to Cincinnati. It was Monday, October 25, 1999. I'm not good with dates, but I remember this one, because as we drove north the radio reported that a Lear Jet carrying golfer Payne Stewart was traveling northwest out of Florida and not responding to ground controllers. As we drove, we heard update after update with the jet's path crossing ours early in the day. We were still driving when the news said that the plane had run out of fuel and crashed in South Dakota. Later it was determined that the jet had depressurized, causing all of the passengers to pass out. It had flown halfway across the continent on autopilot, with military jets flying alongside, unable to help. The mental image of those passengers sleeping in the frigid cold of a depressurized plane, jetting toward their own demise, was one that haunted me for a long time.

After taking a day to regroup from the trip, I got up Wednesday morning and got right to work. I was working my way through some phone calls when I pulled the Memphis gentleman's card from my pocket. On a whim, I dialed the number, thinking, "I have not because I ask not..." At least the first part of that sentence was certainly true.

The next few minutes of conversation would make my head spin and cause great hope and angst for the better part of the next year. Reintroducing myself, I asked if there was any more information he might want regarding our church planting efforts. He asked specifically about our plans for the Hall of Fame building, should we be able to rent it. I told him about the outreach, the worship, all the things that were in our heart.

"What if you don't rent it?" he asked. "What if you buy it?"

I kindly explained that I wasn't sure how I was going to pay the rent, let alone actually buy the building. We were wondering how we were going to buy a few reams of paper for the copier. We certainly hadn't given any thought to buying the building.

"How much would it be to buy?" he pressed. I remembered the owner's representative telling us that it had been on the market at one point for $4 million, so I told him that figure, but again insisted that it wasn't our immediate plan to buy it. If this guy was going to drop a few thousand dollars toward rent, I didn't want to scare him off with the immensity of our real need.

"Here's the deal," he replied. "I'd rather see you buy it than rent it. I'd like to buy it for you."

More than a decade later, I remember that sentence verbatim. It was as if he had said, "Let's take the afternoon and go to the moon." It seemed that fantastic to me—fantastic in the fantasy sense of the word. I needed more information.

"Sir, what do you do for a living?" I asked him. The implication was obvious. What on earth do you do that allows you to drop $4 million on a building sight unseen?

"I invest in foreign currencies," he told me. "I take advantage in minor fluctuations in the market by leveraging large amounts of money, making a tiny bit on each transaction." He continued to talk about what he did while I wrote furiously on my yellow legal pad. Before we said goodbye, I had already plotted my next phone call.

Mark and his wife, Julie, had been part of the church nearly since the beginning. They were both from ministry families and natural leaders. When it was time to assemble an advisory board, he was an easy choice. I liked his understated demeanor and admired his family a great deal. He also happened to be a stock broker with a large bank, and stood a lot better chance at understanding my scribblings than I did.

When he answered the phone, I said, "Mark, listen carefully to me, this is complicated. At least it is to me." Then I proceeded to describe what the the man had told me he did with foreign currencies. When I finished describing it from my notes, I asked the real question I had.

"Is this legal?"

Mark chuckled. He was an analyst to the core. I liked having him in a leadership role because I knew I could always count on him for a brief summary of any situation within seconds.

"It is legal," he said. I breathed a sigh of relief. He continued, "It's also very rare because it's very risky. Is he asking you for money to invest?"

The thought of someone asking us for money made me laugh. The phrase "blood from a turnip" came to mind. "No, not so far," I answered.

"Well, keep talking to him. If he asks for money, run."

The businessman and I did keep talking, often twice a week. With each phone call, I seemed to learn a little more. He had been doing this for years at varying levels and was into his biggest deal ever. When the deal closed, he would be in a position to easily purchase us the Hall of Fame building. He asked for an annual budget for running the building so that he could provide that as well, lest we take on this huge asset and not be able to afford to run it.

I had nothing concrete to tell our congregation. It still sounded too crazy. I did tell the board of our conversations, but quickly reinforced the idea that nothing was certain. We agreed to watch and pray. What else could we do?

With the potential to buy the building in the works, dreaming about how we could use the building seemed to amp up. I often found myself in the parking lot of the building multiple times a day, praying, "Oh God, would You?"

While all of this was taking place, a secondary story also began to evolve. We began a weekly prayer meeting. I was fully engaged, but Kelsey led these meetings—they were her idea and by Saturday night my mind was set on Sunday morning's service.

Those early prayer meetings were not pretty. Think long periods of silence, punctuated by awkward prayers that rambled from "God send revival" to "God save the whales." They were sincere, but they were dry and unfocused. It wasn't our fault—we had never really been taught to pray. Then again, we had never really asked either. Nevertheless, a committed core of ten people would come regularly, and we sensed the pleasure of God on it. I do remember watching Kelsey come alive thinking about prayer and talking about how one day we would have 24/7 prayer in that big brick building we were believing for.

One Saturday night, heading into the next dry prayer meeting, Kelsey proposed an idea. Actually, she mandated it. Until that point, our worship leader would lead us in three or four songs, then put the guitar away. I'm not sure why we did it that way—I guess we had enough American church in us to know the music always went at the front of a gathering. Kelsey—true to form—had another idea.

"Tonight," she announced, "Adam, I want you to play guitar through the entire meeting."

Adam looked at her quickly and asked, "Like...songs?"

"Songs, chords, whatever. Just keep playing."

With that, our prayer model was born. Songs, chords, whatever. Just keep playing. And keep praying.

With the current growth of the prayer movement, there are dozens, if not hundreds, of groups singing and praying across the nation. To be fair, there were probably a lot of people doing it then too—but it was new to us. We would slip from prayer to worship to prayer and back. Our normal hour prayer meeting went an hour and a half. We were shocked at how much difference a little music made in our ability to engage with God.

After a few weeks of praying and worshiping this way, Kelsey confided in me that she was about to tweak the format again. She was weary of our prayer meandering all over the map. It was easier to pray with the music, but it wasn't any more focused than it had been. Prayers for revival mingled with prayers for Aunt Eunice's infected big toe, quickly followed by prayers for God to redeem Hollywood. All worthy requests, but difficult to track and engage with.

I was less critical of her idea—she had obviously been onto something when she added music.

"Tonight," she told me, "we're only going to pray Scripture."

I had set my critical spirit aside, but not too far that I couldn't pick it up again quickly. "Pray Scripture? How on earth do you do that?"

"I'm going to hand every person a Scripture and ask them to pray that Scripture," she said.

"Word for word? How long can you do that?" I countered.

She expounded, "Well, they could pray it word for word, but they don't have to. They could also rephrase it...I just want to use it as a launching pad. Where they go from there is up to them, but let's at least start with something God agrees with."

I shrugged, "Where did you get this idea?"

"It just came to me," she said.

It should be noticed that I can often spot a bad idea a mile away, but I can often miss a good idea right in front of me. This was a very good idea.

Kelsey had gone through the Bible and selected prayers from the Psalms and the New Testament. These bits of Scripture gave people a begininng—a place of reference to pray from. Suddenly our prayers were focused. We were praying in agreement with the Word. We were echoing the thoughts and intentions of Jesus. The Word of God, people's own words, and worship became a beautiful tapestry. Our formerly interminable one hour prayer meetings became enjoyable and easy. Time seemed to fly by.

It should be noticed that the ease of prayer was in marked contrast to the difficulty we were encountering on Sunday mornings. It's not to say that our Sunday services were not enjoyable—there was always a sense of expectancy going into the services—but they took a lot of energy to produce. A rotating team of five of us would show up early to unload chairs and a full sound system. When you have to carry every chair, you begin to think twice about putting out extra chairs. When you don't use those extra chairs week after week, each extra chair mocks you through the service as if to say, "You carried me for nothing."

Meanwhile we still believed the Hall of Fame building to be our permanent home. My calls to the businessman in Memphis continued, with him asking us specifically to pray that money that was being held in off-shore accounts be released, and assuring us that when it was, he would be making the purchase.

Not willing to sit and do nothing, we had extended a proposal to the owner that included our renting the building at a discount in exchange for massive renovations. We figured that once we could pay the purchase price, all those renovations would have made good sense. For the owner of a building in disrepair, it seemed like a golden opportunity, but he seemed remarkably resistant to our gold. This was probably God's protection for us, because even if the owner had said yes, I didn't have a clue where we'd start to raise the necessary funds for renovation.

Every time we drove by the building, we would pray out loud in the car. At our Saturday night gatherings, we would pray. At every board meeting, we would pray. We would pray for the businessman's finances to be released and for favor with the owner of the building, but most of all, we would pray for revival. We would ask God specifically for waves of young people to fill that building with worship around the clock.

After one meeting, I sat talking with one of our board members. We had all the faith in the world for the move of God we were expecting, but honestly, I was beginning to waver in regard to the building. The businessman had been uncharacteristically slow in returning my phone calls that week and it all seemed a little low on momentum. It was as if we'd come to a wall. Still, a fire burned within me to see God be made famous in all this.

Half joking, I suggested to a board member that we should march around the building seven times.

His eyes lit up. "Let's do it!"

One of the most valuable things a church planter can have is someone who will call his bluff. To plant a church is to prophesy something and drag it from the ethereal to the concrete. Sometimes, it's difficult for the pastor to believe his own pronouncements. Our board was great about taking hold of what I'd declared and holding me to it in a loving, encouraging way. Blessed is the leader who has someone who will say, "Let's do it."

By this time, fall had surrendered to winter. The property was generally not maintained, meaning branches, leaves, and snow seemed to cover the edges of the land on all sides.

Regardless, every night for a week, we trudged the perimeter of the 40 acres. Several nights that week, we marched on freshly fallen snow. We prayed our way past the coffee shop. The football stadium. All the way around the building and past the homes I hoped to buy for single moms. At least once we made the march carrying our young sons, because we wanted to look them in the eye as young men and tell them about the trip they'd made. We would return to the front of the building where Jackson had stuck the Post-it Scriptures, and cry out to God for His purposes to come to fruition.

There is no building on earth that is worth the emotional investment we were making, but in reality we weren't investing our hearts in a building. We were pouring our hearts into what we believed God wanted to do—and that included night and day prayer. It included a move of the Holy Spirit. We were inspired to pray because of a building, but we were really praying for all that God would give us.

Over time, our contact with the business owner became less consistent. When I did reach him, he seemed distant. He had little news and even little to ask us to pray about. At one point, I realized I hadn't been able to contact him for several weeks. I began to suspect that all was not as it appeared (I was too young at this point to realize that things are almost never as they appear), and I began to prepare my heart for the truth that the Hall of Fame building may never be ours.

What I discovered was that the dreams God had put in our hearts for prayer, worship, the fire of God, and outreach to others were more real than ever before. I had thought I'd figured out how it would happen, when God was simply giving me a glimpse of how it might happen to see if I'd take the bait and pray. This wasn't about a building, it was about an abandoned life, and we were only beginning to explore the edges of what that could look like.

I had no idea where that exploration would take me from there. We were headed from the Hall of Fame to the desert wilderness and then to Washington, DC, in rapid succession, and it was all connected in a way that we would never have imagined.

TWELVE

The Call to the Wilderness

—〜—

New Year's Eve of 1999, we gathered with the board of SpiritLife for dinner at our home.

I was already fairly certain that we would probably not be getting the Hall of Fame building. I was also more convinced than ever that God was up to something, and I wasn't about to let a building or lack of building influence my faith for those things.

I remember lingering over dinner that night in the final hours of a millennium. Aside from a few concerns that all of our electronics would fry at midnight, we were full of purpose and hope. We prayed that God would do all He had in His heart to do in the year to come.

The spring of 2000, Kelsey announced she wanted to go to Nashville for a conference. Melody, our worship leader's wife, wanted to go along with her.

This was an odd happening—we weren't conference goers and neither family really had the funds to take an extra trip anywhere. "Conference?" I asked, as if I wasn't really sure what the word meant. "Who's speaking?"

Kelsey read several names off the brochure. I didn't recognize any of them. I shrugged.

"I think it's important," she pressed.

I had no interest in a conference, but I also knew that Kelsey had a tendency to be right about these things far more than I was, so the trip was scheduled. The first weekend of May came quickly and Kelsey and Melody headed south. I managed to wrangle our boys while preparing for our regular Sunday morning service, totally unaware of how irregular it would prove to be.

The communication from Kelsey that weekend should have tipped me off that something was up, but perhaps I was too preoccupied with my role as Mr. Mom. Normally when we travel, we stay in very close contact. Her calls were sporadic and short. More specifically, she couldn't seem to give me a summary of the conference.

"How are the services?" I'd ask.

"It's...intense," she would reply.

"How? The music? The preaching?"

"It's...God is moving..." and she would break into tears.

I marked it up to fatigue on her part. After all, I had children to juggle and a sermon to prepare. People were counting on me to deliver on Sunday morning and I didn't have much time to think about a conference featuring people we'd never heard of. Our final call of the weekend took place late Saturday night. She was a wreck, barely able to talk about what had happened in the services. I grew concerned, knowing she had a long drive ahead of her on Sunday. My final instructions to her were, "Sleep well"

Sunday morning, I left the boys with my mother and went about the business of church. Setup went smoothly and by 10 a.m. we were ready to start. I had resisted calling Kelsey's hotel room because I'd hoped she would be able to sleep in. Our little church gathered and started right on time as was our custom. I was big on starting on time—I'd been known to begin a service with no one but the worship band in the room—because I valued people's time and wanted them to get out on time.

Nearing the end of the worship, I heard someone come in the back of the room. Glancing over my shoulder, I saw Kelsey and Melody walk in. It was a little like seeing Santa Claus in July – you're glad to see him, but it's still a shocker. They looked as if they'd gotten up at 5 a.m. and driven like mad women, because in fact they had.

My heart was warmed. "She must have missed me," I thought as she made her way up the center aisle and across the row of seats to take the empty one next to me.

"Welcome home!" I whispered. "I didn't expect you until late today!"

"We got up early and drove home because we have something to share with the church," she told me.

"Uh, now?" I asked. Looking back, I dutifully recognize this as one of the dumber questions of my life. Obviously, she intended on sharing it that morning. There was no reason to get up that early and drive 275 miles if she didn't intend on sharing what God had done.

"Go ahead and preach, but save me some time at the end," she told me. It should be noted that I don't remember a thing I preached that day. Nothing. My guess is that no one else who was there remembers it now either. I do, however, remember Kelsey's portion of the service.

I closed my message about ten minutes before I normally would have, and invited Kelsey and Melody to share. They each took a microphone and turned around like women on fire. They stumbled over their words. They cried. They didn't necessarily communicate with clarity, but they communicated with passion.

Melody and Kelsey had encountered a facet of the Lord in Nashville that we had not previously touched. They had begun to feel what it meant to intercede at a level that we were not reaching in our prayer meetings—not that we didn't want all of what God had, but they'd simply had an encounter we had not yet experienced. Their sudden deep experience was not a condemnation on our efforts until then. In fact, what happened to them in Nashville was probably partially the result of leaning into God during all those months of dry prayer meetings.

In addition to speaking about intercession, they told us, "There is an event in September entitled TheCall. Lou Engle is calling an entire nation to fast and pray in Washington, DC, on Labor Day weekend—we all need to get there."

I remember chuckling at her saying "get there" as if it were the Oregon Trail. I figured we'd think about it and decide later. Kelsey had already decided. We were going. After church, a torrent of words came out of her as she was able to process the weekend a little more fully.

"We need to take the entire church. This is the most significant gathering in our lifetime," she insisted. "Lou is calling the nation to pray and fast on the same weekend as this thing called... Burning...Man?"

That triggered a memory somewhere. I'd heard about an event in the desert called Burning Man but my understanding of it was pretty limited.

"Burning Man is the largest pagan gathering in the world. Thousands of people party around a 70 foot tall effigy of a man and then burn him to the ground. They dare God to answer them. We are going to DC the same weekend," she explained, "to ask God to answer us. It will be Elijah and the prophets of Baal all over again."

I stared at my wife. She was serious. And something inside me told me she was right.

Two weeks later, we were invited to Steve and Janie Sjogren's home. Steve and I had become unlikely buddies, the pastor of the megachurch and the planter of the unintentionally micro-church.

Sitting there over Cincinnati's legendary Donato's Pizza, we shared the news about TheCall. Mingled in between bites of pizza, we told Steve and Janie what we had heard. Burning Man. TheCall.

Elijah and the prophets of Baal. We were excited about going to DC to pray with other believers from across the nation.

Little did I know the impact of Steve's next sentence. If I knew then what I know now, I could have seen it coming, but I didn't. It came out of nowhere, but it was pointed directly at us. Steve has a gift of viewing things at a 45 degree angle from the rest of the world. He's not oppositional, as if he were 180 degrees. He's just canted to one side like the head of the dog on the RCA label. One ear cocked, a quizzical look on his face.

"I think you should go to Burning Man," he said with a smile. I would learn later that he had a habit of delivering his craziest ideas with a wide smile. He found it disarmed people. He once told me, "It's hard to get angry at a smiling guy…"

I wasn't angry at him. I just thought he was nuts. I laughed at him and reached for another piece of pizza.

His voice lowered, "I'm serious."

I glanced at Janie to see if she was reaching for his medication. Instead, she was just gazing at him adoringly. She seemed to enjoy his particular brand of crazy; and at the moment, he was at the pinnacle.

He was obviously waiting for a reaction, so I reacted. "That's nuts," I said flatly.

Steve pressed, "TheCall sounds great. I bet there will be a ton of Christians there. I bet there won't be many Christians at Burning Man. I think you ought to go to Burning Man."

I remember the entire exchange in great detail, but I remember almost nothing after that moment. My head was swimming with the idea of a crazy man…not because I was offended, but because I feared he might be right.

Over the next several nights, I lay in bed unable to sleep. I believed the Lord was speaking and had to admit I was more afraid of missing Him than I was afraid of obeying Him. I finally surrendered to the Lord and admitted Steve was right. The next morning, I called him.

"Steve, you're right," I said. "Let's go to Burning Man."

"Oh, I'm not going to Burning Man. You are," he replied. "Me? No way. That's crazy."

It is one thing to submit to the Lord contingent on someone else going with you. It's an entirely different thing to determine to submit on your own. After further conversation with Kelsey, we both agreed that I was to go. My research started that day.

What I learned was startling, particularly to a suburban Cincinnati pastor. Burning Man—more formally titled The Burning Man Arts Festival—was nearly twenty years old at that time. About 30,000 people would gather on a dry lakebed in remote Nevada for a week of parties and often lewd behavior. Drugs were not the main attraction but they certainly moved freely through the crowd, who clamored for radical self-expression and radical self-reliance.

The organizers of Burning Man had intentionally made it difficult to participate. The word "remote" does not do the location justice. The dry lakebed is 12 by 15 miles—a vast expanse that resembles a dirt parking lot. The featureless alkali surface is so inhospitable that bugs do not live there. There is no electricity. No water. No sanitation. No cell phone service. Nothing is provided and a ticket must be purchased. In bold letters, the back of the ticket says "You may die at this event." It is not exaggerating. Burning Man is not for the faint of heart.

Kelsey and I knew that this trip was engaging with spiritual powers to a degree we'd never encountered before. We quickly agreed that a forty day fast was in order. It should be noted that we had little to no experience in fasting for more than a day or two.

Many people believe that the hardest sort of fast to do is to eat nothing and drink only water. In reality, over time, your body adjusts to this and while you will grow weak and hunger will wane, it's not as bad as it could be. In our ignorance, we set a course for ourselves and our team that was actually worse. We ate very small portions of beans or rice on Monday, Wednesday, and Friday. On

Tuesday, Thursday, and Saturday, we ate nothing and drank only juice. On Sundays, we drank only water. Thinking we were charting an easier course by taking in some calories, we simply forced our body into an on-again, off-again metabolic mess.

We also determined to meet nightly with Melody, the young woman Kelsey had gone to Nashville with, and her husband, Adam. Adam was our church's worship leader and was committed to the Burning Man trip with me. Fasting as a group made it far easier to stay committed, especially knowing we'd see each other every night.

I'm not sure what I expected from those nightly meetings, but they fell short—at least initially. We would sit and stare at one another, hungry for God, but just as hungry if not hungrier for a good meal. Our prayers were demure. We had zero sense of hearing from the Lord once we started. That went on for twenty-one days. On that twenty-first day, something shifted. We began to dream. We began to hear from God. Our prayer times became alive. Our fasting, weak and grumpy as it was, somehow grabbed God's heart and He answered us. For the final nineteen days, we enjoyed what felt like the manifest presence of God as we would gather for two hours in our living room.

We felt the Lord speak clearly about this trip—going to Burning Man as a prophetic witness was important for us. For Burning Man. For TheCall. Kelsey felt impressed to pray for rain in the desert—something that almost never happened. We cried for rain in the desert and rain on our hard hearts. By the end of the fast, my weight had dropped from 135 pounds to 117 pounds. I looked so hollow that strangers regularly offered me help opening doors. I could sit in 90 degree heat and I felt as if it were winter. But my heart was alive and full of faith.

Looking back, I realize what happened. In the decision to go to Burning Man and the fast that followed, I was able to disconnect my belief that God wanted to do something from the Hall of

Fame where I thought He wanted to do it. To use a popular phrase in a new way, my faith left the building.

We timed our fast to end two weeks before Burning Man to enable us to better prepare. In those two weeks, we rented an RV, prepared wilderness camping gear, and ordered 5,000 bottles of water to be delivered in Reno, Nevada, the city nearest the dry lakebed where Burning Man was held. We figured that if you were going into a strange crowd it would be best to bring a gift, and what better gift to bring to the desert than water? Actually, Sjogren had suggested loin cloths. We all laughed, but once we got there, we realized that he may have been on to something.

When the time came to leave for the desert, the RV was backed into our driveway and packed full of food. As we gathered in the driveway to say goodbye to our wives, Kelsey picked up five smooth stones from our yard. As they prayed over us, she gave us each a smooth stone and said, "You're going to need these—you guys are Davids going up against Goliath." We tucked the stones in our pockets, climbed on board the RV, and headed out. Little did we know the role those little Jesus rocks would play in the desert.

Pointing our RV west on the highway with four other men who had spent forty days fasting, full of faith and ready for anything, there was a smile on my face and joy in my heart. I'd never felt so in the very center of what God told me to do.

Then my cell phone rang.

The person on the other end claimed to be a "high level intercessor." This made a big impression on me at the time, because that sort of language was all new to me. More than a decade later, I realize that no one ever introduces themselves as a low level intercessor, but back then, I was impressed.

"Pastor Bohlender," she asked. This was probably my first clue she was void of a prophetic spirit. Technically, I was a pastor, but it was a title I'd never utilized. I had to think for a moment before I realized she meant me.

"Yes," I shouted over the roar of the RV.

"I am a high level intercessor for (insert name of well-known prophetic speaker here)." Then she paused, presumably for my reaction.

"Okay," I shouted. I wasn't trying to be rude. I really couldn't hear very well in the RV.

"We understand that you are going to the Burning Man event?" she asked.

"Yes, we are on our way."

"Ok, I'm glad I caught you. I was just speaking to the Lord, and He told me to tell you that your team is overconfident and full of pride."

Instinctively I glanced in the overhead mirror at the four guys in the RV. Their eyes were sunken in from fasting. They had left their families and put up their own cash to do this. They were going into uncharted waters. We might have been ignorant, but we knew we were ignorant. It petrified us, but we were more scared of disobedience than we were failure. Ordinarily, I would have taken this very seriously, but given what I knew, I chalked it up to an overzealous high level intercessor.

I looked back out the windshield, and replied into the phone, "Okay. Thanks."

She continued, "I just wanted you to know."

I firmed up my one handed grip on the steering wheel and repeated, "Okay. Thanks."

The high level intercessor hung up. I closed the phone. Someone asked, "Who was that?"

I replied, "Nobody," and kept driving.

The team was far from perfect, but the one thing we were not was overconfident. If she would have called and said we were freaking out, I would have pulled over and taken notes, because I would have recognized the voice of God.

We knew how to preach. We knew how to sing. We even learned how to fast. We had no clue how to wander into thousands of blatant pagans and walk out the other side.

THIRTEEN

Send the Rain

—⚏—

Everyone should load their friends into an RV and drive cross country nonstop once in their life. It is an experience that will stretch them. That said, once is probably enough for a lifetime. The idea of traveling by RV as a fun, restful way to see the country was quickly abandoned when we realized that our ride, pulling a heavy trailer, was more like being trapped in a small apartment during a 2,200 mile earthquake. Everything rattled, wind roared, the engine whined. It was so loud that conversation was almost impossible. Once we got out of the parking lot and onto the highway, it was even louder.

Against all odds—our own ineptitude, trailer lights that refused to work, and the winds of the Midwest—we managed to get to Reno in about forty hours. It is a feat I am not eager to repeat. We found our way to a campground we planned to use as a base for twenty-four hours as we gathered final supplies.

We decided that a gift of 5,000 bottles would be needed to make some sort of impact. Not wanting to carry 5,000 bottles of water across the country, we had traveled with our trailer nearly empty, and had ordered water to be delivered to a church in Reno.

I should have anticipated a problem when, upon asking the water company, "How much space do 5,000 bottles of water take?" their response was to ask me how much space I had. When I described the 5' x 8' trailer we were bringing, they assured me that it would fit. I think it had more to do with making the sale than it did with making the water fit.

Breaking camp the morning we planned to head out to the desert, we drove to the church in anticipation of easily loading 5,000 bottles of water into our trailer and motoring on. Spirits were high, resolution was strong, and we were excited. Then we turned the corner into the church and I saw the stockpile of water. Our trailer had room for about one and a half pallets of water. Sitting there on the church loading dock were nearly four.

Deciding to do our best to try and make it work, we quickly loaded the trailer full. It did not begin to swallow all of the cases of water bottles. In fact, once full, the tires of the trailer splayed out at odd angles and the trailer rested firmly on its frame rails. It was overloaded—and the majority of our water still sat on the dock. In the end, we offloaded some of the water to make the trailer safe, moved lighter groceries from the RV to the trailer, then filled every crevice of the RV—every cabinet, every shelf, all the floor space, with cases of water. When we were done, we had about thirty cases left. On a whim, we bungeed them to the roof of the RV.

Then we noticed that the RV itself was sitting with its fenders directly on the back tires. For a moment, I panicked. I wondered if we were defeated. Had we come this far, spent this much, and worked so hard to be thwarted by something as basic as too much cargo? Then it occurred to me—along with 5,000 bottles of water, five men and a ton of camping gear, we were carrying a full tank of water on the RV. I ordered the tank plugs pulled and we jettisoned the 100 gallons of water in the tank. At over eight pounds per gallon, we trimmed 800 pounds of weight and gained about an inch of clearance off the fenders. Declaring this to be safe (based on zero research), we drove for the desert.

The 120 miles from Reno to the Black Rock Desert may have been the longest of my life. We had prayed and fasted all summer for this but we really didn't know what to expect. We weren't sure what our reception would be or even how to approach Burning Man attendees, or Burners, as they call themselves.

Finding a sign directing us to pull off the highway, we eased the water-laden rig off the shoulder and on to a dry lakebed. We joined a convoy of hippies, techies, and oddballs driving RVs, VW vans, rental trucks, sedans, and even motorcycles. Behind us, a man drove a rare Mercedes MOG truck. In front of us, there was a long white limousine...with sunbathers on the roof. With tension high, we approached the six lane gate where greeters, in (and out) of various costumes, were checking tickets and welcoming people. We were warmly welcomed and our RV was quickly searched for stow aways. Of course, every cabinet or storage area they opened was full of water.

"Are you guys really thirsty?" the greeter asked.

"Uh..." I stammered. "We brought some extra water..."

The greeter grinned and said, "I see that." In light of all that would come through the gate of Burning Man that day, five guys with a thousand bottles of water for each of them did not even register on the strange-o-meter.

Once inside the city, we went to work setting up our cases of water as a sort of wall around the front of the RV. It almost felt like the cowboys fortifying against the Indians. Just then, a native rode up on a bike. He was wearing bike shorts and a paper-mache goat's head mask. I greeted him and handed him a bottle of water. As he took the cap off the water, he pushed his mask up to the top of his head to allow himself to drink.

Eyeing our stash of water, he asked, "Why are you guys doing this?"

"Doing what?" I replied, as if we regularly wandered out into thousands of pagans with an RV full of water.

"Giving away water. Why are you giving away water?" he pressed.

There are times in life where you get into situations you just haven't thought through. For all of our preparations, all our spreadsheets, all of our overcoming the craziest of situations, this was one question I hadn't considered. Of course, I knew why we were doing it, but I hadn't thought through explaining it to a man in a goat's head mask.

I looked straight at him and said, "We're doing this as a prophetic declaration of what God wants to do in your life. He wants to bring water to the dry places inside you. He's water in the desert."

That conversation later led to an open door to pray for this young man, who was as dry in spirit as he was in the flesh. The answer I gave—seemingly off the top of my head—became our mantra. We must have repeated it a thousand times over the next few days. A God of pews and hymnals did not make sense to these people, but a God that refreshed like water in the desert was just what they were looking for.

The next few days at Burning Man was like the Theatre of the Absurd. We would wander back and forth between profound discussions and prayer times with broken people and watching a plumber and his two helpers assemble and demonstrate their homemade roller coaster. Then, we'd go back to talking and praying with people, only to take a break later to wander out to the seventy foot tall Burning Man where thousands danced in a circle around his neon and wood frame. At times it was lighthearted and fun, but it often felt sinister. It was especially so at night, as we'd climb on the roof of the RV to see a thousand campfires around us in the desert and hear the techno music echoing off the Black Rock Range. We were never unaware that we were in a real spiritual battle.

Back at home, Kelsey had formed a prayer team that prayed around the clock for us. In addition to their own prayer hours, they would gather each night and pray for our safety, for wisdom, and for prophetic insight. Specifically, they prayed that God would show His power by rain. Meanwhile, we wandered the desert praying for people and warning them "Rain is coming."

I'd be lying if I told you that I completely believed it. I wanted to believe it, but it just seemed too fantastic. The Black Rock Desert is just what you'd imagine—dry as a bone. It's so dry that you can work most of the day in the hot sun without breaking a sweat. A moist wipe pulled from the pack will become dry as tissue paper inside a few minutes. Several times a day dust storms blow through that reduce visibility to a few feet or less. Rain seemed so unlikely that it was easier to rely on the spiritual interpretation.

Late in the week, we broke camp to head home and then on to Washington, DC, for TheCall. We had made dear friends with this strange tribe. I'd even done an interview for a documentary. The filmmaker asked to interview us based on our extravagant gift of water, but as I shared how we were bringing the message of Jesus to the playa, both she and members of her crew found their eyes filling with tears. Even as we packed, though, we spoke of rain. Our Burning Man neighbors chuckled. At Burning Man, five Christians muttering about a coming rain in the desert is the strangest thing they had seen.

Forty-five minutes later, as we neared the interstate and were able to pick up a cell phone signal, I called Kelsey. She excitedly told me of their intense nightly prayer meetings. I tried to relate to her the story of the goat-head boy or the propane tank explosions. While we eagerly talked over one another, grateful to hear the others' voice, out of nowhere huge black clouds rolled in from the south. Before I could even tell her what I was seeing, the RV was pelted with the largest rain drops imaginable. It was deafening in the RV as the wipers struggled to keep up with the torrent. I'm not sure what it sounded like on Kelsey's end, but even the roar of the rain was drowned out in the RV as five very dusty, very tired men roared "Yeaaaaaaahhhh God!" at the top of their lungs.

On our return trip exhaustion had set in, causing us to swap out driving in short two hour shifts. We pulled into Omaha about thirty hours after we left the Black Rock Desert to see the front of the LIFE section of the *USA Today* declaring, "Thousands Leave Burning Man Because of Rain."

It should be clarified that we were not praying against people. We were praying for people—and that God would show His power in a unique way. We fell in love with the people who called themselves Burners, and formed good friendships that continue to this day. We also learned that God will fight for those who take a bold step on His behalf.

With one overnight stop in our own beds in Cincinnati, we once again loaded up and headed east to Washington, DC, for TheCall DC It was an event as dramatic as anything we'd seen in the desert.

We spent the night before TheCall in the Phoenix Hotel on Capitol Hill. We were gathered there with most of our little church, including Kelsey's prayer team.

During the time we were gone, their prayer meetings had grown more and more intense. What had started as a simple, "Oh God, send rain," had evolved into a wild, circular Native American, drum-driven prayer dance each night. I was a little amazed at it myself.

Emboldened by God's answering their prayer for rain in the desert, they determined not to break their streak of praying for God to show His power. Kelsey grabbed a CD player and scouted a place for their prayer meeting. They found a vacant hotel ball-room and commandeered it. Under low lights, they hit play on the CD and began to pray, sing, and dance their rain dance for Jesus. In the height of their prayer dance fury, a hotel steward poked his head in to see what all the commotion was about. Apparently, the sight of six white Midwesterners doing a rain dance was more than he had time for because he quickly shut the door and did not return.

September 2, 2000, was among the most signficant days of my life. So eager and full of anticipation of what God might do, we made our way to the National Mall in Washington, DC, a full forty minutes before the 6 a.m. start. We were shocked to find that tens of thousands of others had the same idea. They were streaming out of the Metro stations, unloading from bus stops, and walking to The Mall from all directions in DC that morning. Even before arriving on The Mall we had become part of a surging sea of people.

The sun rises over the city about 6:30 a.m. in September. With it barely a hint of pink behind the Capitol building, the lights came up on the stage and gave us first sight of two things. One was a massive banner with an arrow pointed upward. It signified exactly what this day was about. The other thing we noticed was just how many people were already on The Mall. The crowd stretched back as far as the eye could see, even at that hour. We were hit with a wall of sound that marked me forever as a band began with the lyrics, "Did you feel the mountains tremble? Did you hear the oceans roar, when the people rose to sing of Jesus Christ the risen Lord?"

I found my way over to a tree on the north side of the mall and wept. Kelsey came over to find me there and asked, "Are you okay?" I was not given to such outbursts. Over a decade later, I still can't fully describe what I was feeling. The closest I can come is to say that after standing in the desert among tens of thousands who would shake their fist at God, to stand among a greater throng declaring His worth was like going from a hot tub into a cold pool of water. The difference was almost shocking.

The crowd gathered there was a mishmash of evangelicals, charismatics, and those unaware of the expectation that they declare a major. Blue-haired ladies mixed with blue-haired teenagers. Hundreds of students from the Brownsville School of Ministry volunteered in their orange shirts. The event was completely void of merchandising. There was a book station far back in the crowd, but the books were being given away. I finally found a t-shirt to buy a good distance from the stage—a haunting black and white photo of young adults holding a sign that said "Will Work for Revolution." Over a decade later, I still run into people who have one of those shirts. They're reluctant to part with it. It means something to them.

The day of TheCall held more than a few moments that are seared into my heart. I remember Michael W. Smith quietly taking the stage and launching into the haunting "This is Your Time," recounting the recent high school martyrs from Columbine.

At one point the stage flooded with Native American drummers who pounded on huge drums, which led Kelsey and her radical band of intercessors to jump up for a wild, impromptu rain dance on the National Mall. After the incident in the hotel the night before, this seemed like a perfectly natural thing to do.

Under the hot sun, Lou Engle took the microphone to pray for those who were attending Burning Man that day. His gravelly voice roared, "They're burning a man in the desert tonight." I stood there with dust from the playa on my Doc Martins. I had intentionally worn them that day because I wanted the same shoes that had seen the dust of Burning Man to stand there on The Mall. A man burned in the desert, but a Man burned on The Mall and He drew all men unto Himself. I was declaring which Man I was for that day.

As the day came to a close, something remarkable happened. From the west, across the Potomac, clouds formed and rain began to fall on The Mall. It started as a light sprinkle—the kind people are hesitant to respond to, as if acknowledging the rain makes it real. Ignore it and maybe it will pass...but we couldn't ignore it. This rain was not an inconvenience. This was a sign.

As a group—men who'd attended Burning Man, the prayer team who had held the line night after night, extended families—we stood with hands upraised, faces turned upward, rain pelting our faces, melding with tears and falling down to the dry cracks in the earth. For a moment, I took my eyes from heaven to see my two little boys dancing wildly in the mud. They each wore little orange and white tie-died t-shirts that Kelsey had hand lettered with the words "Elijah was a boy just like me." Truer words were never before printed on a t-shirt.

There is a kiss from God for those who recklessly throw themselves at Him. In our case, it came in the form of a rain shower. The rain that fell that day—an echo of that which had fallen on the desert a few days earlier—was a sign and a wonder in our hearts, assuring us that we had been heard on high and emboldening us to ask big of a big God.

The fast the summer of 2000, Burning Man, TheCall—it was all the beginning of hearing from heaven more clearly than we ever had before. It was the beginning of dreaming about more of God than I ever suspected existed. And it was probably the death knell to SpiritLife Community Church.

FOURTEEN

Redefining Weird

—⚏—

I remember hearing stories of fellow Bible college students once we all scattered to the wind. This being prior to the Internet, bits of info flew too and fro via hard copy letters and phone calls. One of my favorite stories was about a fellow student who, upon taking a pastorate in a small southern town, immediately took the church van to the local paint shop and had it lettered—in huge letters that could not be missed—"The Most Exciting Church in Town."

He told me about this as we both served as counselors in a youth camp the first year we lived in Tennesse. He was still quite jazzed about it. I remember thinking, "Dude, that's a lot of pressure." It's one thing to say, "We show up, God shows up, what happens happens..." but, "the most exciting church in town" was a promise I was never going to make.

I am suspicious of pastors and ministries that try to promise that the next church service will be the greatest, the most defining, the one you can't afford to miss. I am generally for church attendance, but I have found that churches are best suited as places to be challenged. Actual change usually happens later in the week, like on a Tuesday, when your world goes pear shaped and you need to respond in a godly manner.

Because of this perspective, I don't believe there are many defining church services. There can't be—there are too many services for a group of people to constantly be redefined. The congregation that has their identity radically changed every week is probably suffering from some sort of disorder.

Having said all that, the Sunday that followed TheCall was, in a sense, defining. Not necessarily for the church, but certainly for me. I had been to the desert, I had been to TheCall, and my inner man was churning with thoughts and impressions. Some were God's, some were mine, and in some glorious instances, they were both. Years later I remember hearing Mike Bickle relay a story about how a long time church member once told him, "I had no idea what you were talking about back in those years." Mike replied that he was fine with that, because he was preaching to himself, declaring what he was about. Sunday, September 10, 2000, I threw down a gauntlet before my church, myself, and my God.

As I said earlier, I don't like titles, but I remember the title of that message. It was "The Redefinition of My Personal Concept of Weird." I'm not sure if it was the title or the content, but for some reason it struck a chord and can be found referenced in a number of places online (usually in part, sometimes incorrectly, and with the wrong date). In a very strange turn of events, a few months later, the Burning Man organization actually discovered the transcript and linked it to their Jack Rabbit Speaks, an email list of thousands of Burners and would-be Burners, causing a massive amount of Internet traffic to our fledgling church website, mostly from Burners who were looking to process their own spiritual experiences of Burning Man.

That Sunday, I got up and preached my guts out. It has proven to be a seminal message for me.

I'll save you the hunting and wondering if you're seeing the accurate version by giving you the sermon's six points, along with a line or two of explanation, some from the transcripts I found, and some editorializing from ten plus years of interpretation.

I started the message by recapping our trip and what I felt on The Mall in DC, then announced that I had redefined my personal concept of weird for the following reasons.

1) I no longer find it weird that Burning Man thrives in a harsh setting with no advertising budget.

Prior to traveling to Nevada for The Burn, we couldn't imagine how they would get multiple thousands of people to do this very expensive thing without any normal sense of promotion. There is no Burning Man advertising campaign. It is difficult to get accurate information about. Yet each year the event grows (at the time of this writing, it's topping 50,000 souls). What I found at the event was a temporary attempt at authentic community that touched a place in people's souls, which the church was largely ignoring.

2) I do find it weird that the church strives to convenience people when people really thrive on challenge.

We were planting a church in a season when all around us, the model being promoted was a hardcore, seeker-sensitive one. We were being told that if we didn't make people comfortable—in fact, if we didn't focus on people's comfort—that our church was doomed. At Burning Man I realized that people were leaning hard into a challenge, not an easy chair. I grew convicted by my own slack approach to challenging the people God had given me. I was doing them a massive disservice.

3) I no longer find it weird when people express themselves in ways I never thought of.

I grew up in North Dakota. NoDaks are the salt of the earth. You want one in your fox hole when it hits the fan because they'll be there for you. They'll give you their last round of ammo. And they'll make you a hot dish to go with it. They are not, by and large, known for their creativity. There are only so many ways to shovel snow.

At Burning Man, I was struck by the vast amount of creativity. In that setting, creativity wasn't just entertainment—it was existence. The playa is the largest art canvas in the world. It could even drive a North Dakotan to create. It is fraught with the tension of what-if. What if we painted that? What if we mounted it on a boom? What if we lit it on fire? Would people come see it burn?

It also changed our mind about what might be possible. We saw a homemade roller coaster. I played on a 70 foot long teeter-totter. We witnessed the florescent-lit, gauze-walled Church of Funk. As Adam, our worship leader, said, "Before Burning Man, I might have said, 'Cool PowerPoint slide.' Now, I'm more likely to think, 'Wow—who mounted a boat on the roof of that bus?'"

It was not just that they were outside the box. They'd dismantled the box, burned half of it, put wheels on the other half and were using it as a mountain scooter to race down ski runs. I had a newfound admiration for fabrication.

4) I find it weird that the church world appears to have been made from a cookie cutter.

Serving primarily a church of techies, I'd found it helpful to read things like *Wired* and *Fast Company*. I returned from Burning Man to find a *Fast Company* feature on a traveling salesman who found normalcy on the road by attending a worship service every weekend he was away from his family. While his dedication was beautiful, his reasoning was this: "No matter what city I am in, if I go to church, I get essentially the same experience."

That seemed whacked up to me. Was it really a good thing that you could walk into any church coast to coast and not expect to be surprised? How did the body of Christ convert to the business plan of Starbucks? Surely creative people serving a creative God could find a way to express their love to one another in something more dynamic than a spiritual vanilla latte.

As long as I've been tracking the trends, the church has run from one expression to the other, based on what has worked for a specific megachurch—never mind that the architect of that megachurch was uniquely wired to do things that specific way. The talented souls leading those megachurches have failed to resist the idea that they've fallen into a new way of doing things, and that they are uniquely suited to relay that information to a huge number of consumers, er, churches who want to do exactly the same thing and get the exact same results.

The cycle of church success, church product development, church marketing, and church replication was invented by well-meaning, God-fearing people, but stripped the church of the dignity of creativity and robbed God of the sort of finger painting that any parent loves to hang on the fridge.

5) I no longer find it weird that people will go to great lengths to escape their reality.

We noticed something quickly at Burning Man. Adam, our worship leader, was gifted at conversation with these folks. I could pour cold water on a conversation more quickly than you could imagine. The difference? Our approach. Adam would engage people on the basis of what they wanted to be or do. He'd ask them questions about what they thought or felt. They would expound at great length about their dreams and hopes.

Then I'd ask, "So, what do you do back in the real world?"

Conversation over. Pressed about what I would have called the real world, these creative types would just shut down.

I wasn't trying to kill the moment, but I did. And I did it with a sincere heart. These people were fascinating. I wanted to know what they did for a living, how they lived, that sort of thing. I wanted to define them by the sorts of terms that most people define themselves by because it would have enabled me to categorize them easily...but they resisted categorization. They did not come to be boxed in. Instead, they had come hundreds or thousands of miles to escape that, and my pestering questions only yanked them back to an unsatisfying existence. If reality were cutting it for them, they would have stayed there.

6) I find it weird that so many believers are satisfied with their present reality.

Unbelievers generally have a better grip on the idea of pilgrimage than believers do. They understand that change is usually found over the horizon, and one needs to go somewhere to find it.

In the proliferation of talk about a personal God, we have become consumed with the idea of Him meeting us where we are, even when where we are is a total mess. Burners looking for an experience were willing to escape their present reality to find one. I'm not sure the church is up for that.

Understand, I do not dislike the church. I was raised in the church and have massive appreciation for it historically, socially, and theologically. The church has mattered in history, matters in the present, and will matter in the future.

That said, most of these things are true in spite of the church's best efforts. The American fast food church has so simplified the intricacies of God that we're a hand wave and a signature away from the promise of eternal life, which is then delivered in the form of a hectic but unfulfilled church schedule, as if God so loved the world that He made them busy.

As the sheep are kept running to and fro, most of them fail to realize that they never actually leave the corral. They are moving fast and furious, but not far. Effort is being exerted, but work is not getting done. When they stop for a moment to catch their breath, the ornery ones ask, "Is this all there is?" The true Shepherd assures them, "No...there is more."

Isaiah 43:18-19 says:
Forget the former things, do not dwell on the past. See, I am doing a new thing! Do you not perceive it? I am making a way in the desert and streams in the wasteland.

I returned from Burning Man and TheCall pretty dismayed with the church, upper and lowercase. I believed more deeply than ever that the answers to all of humanity's needs were found within her creeds, but not within her walls, and yet I had spent the better part of the past several years trying to get people inside those walls so they could stand and I could count them.

I was very responsible for the church we had built, and after seeing what I had seen the previous few weeks, I had to admit I was sick of it. As near as I can find from the scattered Internet notes, the final words of my sermon that Sunday were these:

I am sick of our reality, and am so committed to seeing the streams God wants to pour into our lives that I plan to be impossible to be around until we see it…and if that's weird, sign me up.

Phrases like "I plan to be impossible to be around…" are not the stuff that tender sermon endings are made of. I hadn't really planned on throwing down a gauntlet. In fact, I wasn't sure that I had…but it certainly felt like it. And I'd thrown it down in front of myself, of all people.

SpiritLife was an unconventional church in a number of ways. We didn't really have the traditional howdy-and-shake-hands time with the pastor at the door as people left. Most weeks we were meeting in temporary facilities and had to tear down our entire PA system, so if you wanted a moment with the pastor, you needed to come to the front and, preferably, help haul gear. It was a counsel and carry session.

That Sunday, after the final amen, I was coiling audio cable in neat loops when the first person approached me. Over ten years later, I am still grateful for her honesty.

"You just scared me," she said.

"I did?" As I said before, I was kind of preaching to myself. And I had suspected my preaching might disappoint people, but I never thought of myself as scary.

"Yes, you did. What you were preaching about could bring a lot of the people like that…" her voice trailed off.

"Like who?" I pressed. I knew what she was getting at, but sometimes it's good to say things out loud.

"I'm not really sure. Like them. Like those people you met at Burning Man. I've got to be honest. I am petrified of that. I hate to admit it, but I'm not sure how to relate to them, or if I could even welcome them if they come."

Years later, as I type this on my computer, it's difficult to capture the tenderness of the conversation. This person wasn't protesting. She was being very vulnerable. She wasn't exactly asking for help, but she was certainly acknowledging her own personal hesitancy in embracing the sort of Christianity I was talking about.

I was proposing something very different—adhering to the creeds of the church, but somehow obliterating the walls. I couldn't blame people for being a little panicky. This was a new idea to me, and I was the one proposing it.

I was preaching thoughts that were only days old for me. It was ridiculous to think that people could go from zero to sixty in one sermon. My journey had been far longer than that, and I had my own black and blue marks, and I'd have more before this was all over. I didn't necessarily expect a pat on the back and an assurance that anyone was with me. I wasn't even sure I could go where I wanted to go, much less lead others.

No one else approached me that Sunday. Some may have avoided me. There was certainly a sobriety as we packed up the trailer with our chairs and audio system. I do remember shaking my head as people referred to putting the church on the trailer. Of course I knew what they meant, but the fact that those sorts of comments were becoming part of our landscape told me the change I wanted so badly might kill us all.

Sermons in subsequent weeks were rather surly. It seemed that each week I identified one more thing wrong with myself and crafted a message to attempt to blast it out of me. I attacked hypocrisy, laziness, lethargy, lack of love, and a host of other things that plagued the church as a whole, and this pastor in particular. Again, these were far more my problems than theirs.

Some attendees noticed a difference. They certainly noticed that I cared less about the few programs we were running during the week. They noticed that while I had shaved my head for the Burning Man trip, I unexpectedly kept it shaved when I got home. One person asked, "Are you doing this for shock value?"

I smiled but shook my head no. An honest answer would have been, "I'm trying to shock myself into action."

A few weeks later, I took yet another step outside of everyone's comfort zone including my own. I was sitting in a Barnes & Noble, waiting for the church board to arrive for a meeting. If the meeting were to go as the others, we would review finances, talk a little about logistics, I would lament the slow growth of the congregation, they would assure me that they knew I was trying hard, and we'd dismiss. The ritual took about ninety minutes.

Sitting there fully knowing what to expect saddened my heart. Not because of the board themselves—they were excellent men of God who were only going where I was leading them (which wasn't far). I was frustrated with myself. Frustrated that I was building the church that I deserved—one populated with warm-hearted, well-meaning people, but not the dangerous entity that I had imagined. I'd become so consumed with the entity that I was losing sight of the mission.

I was also living under a great deal of fear of men. Even then I knew this was unwarranted. My church leaders were nothing but kind and supportive. The denomination, while puzzled by me, hadn't offered any real resistance. I was afraid of what people thought even when no one was sharing contrary thoughts with me. It was a stronghold completely rooted in my own false perceptions and my tendency to entertain worry.

In that moment, I heard the Lord in a way that has only happened a handful of times. I would love to hear this clearly on a daily basis, but I don't. As I sat at that empty table waiting for the board to join me, I heard God say, "I want you to do something that no one will understand, and then I want you to resist the temptation to explain yourself. You need to break the fear of man by doing something that you know will be questioned...and you need to just let it be."

Instantly, I knew what that meant. For perhaps the first time in my life, I acted in robot-like obedience. The word was so clear—and the understanding so specific—that I was experiencing an element of the fear of the Lord over this. I slid back from my seat, walked out to my car and drove across the street to a mall. Walking into the mall, I went to the first jewelry store I could find, plunked down a debit card, and had them pierce my left ear.

It wasn't a fashion statement. It wasn't an act of rebellion. It was an act of obedience—or at least the first part of one. Actually, the piercing was the easy part. It was the not explaining myself that was going to be difficult, because those who fear man desperately want to explain themselves.

Once gathered back at the meeting, my board noticed immediately, but didn't ask the obvious question, "What did you do that for?" Instead, we held our predictable meeting. We said goodbye, and as we walked out, one of them held the door open for me. As I walked by, he smiled and said, "Uh, nice earring." It wasn't sarcastic. It was just an attempt to acknowledge the obvious—that my ear was bright red, obviously recently pierced, and it hadn't been referred to in the meeting.

It killed me not to explain myself. In retrospect, I believe that was God's intent. The killing began that day and continues today.

As a side note, I still wear an earring. In fact, I have both ears pierced now and one sports a second hole. The first was a radical challenge to my fear of man. The second and third marked significant anniversaries. It's funny what takes so much courage to do the first time becomes commonplace the next. Perhaps courage truly has accumulative qualities.

FIFTEEN

Wave after Wave

—ʍ—

Having redefined my concept of weird, and finding much of what I'd committed to building seemed to fall well within that catagory, I now set out to find my new normal. I wasn't sure where Burning Man, TheCall, and this strange sense of setting myself apart was leading, but it certainly wasn't inviting me to sit still.

The summer leading into those events had been marked with prayer and fasting. In the process of killing our flesh, we'd never felt so alive. Some of our joy, though, was tied to an expiration date. The fast was finite, even if forty days seemed like eternity. Our prayers for God to move at Burning Man and TheCall were connected to a date on the calendar. He'd met us in those places, but now what?

It was in this season that SpiritLife moved its services again, this time from an apartment complex clubhouse to the building owned by the deaf congregation that I mentioned earlier. To be quite honest, I'm not sure what the motivation was. The rent was not outrageous, so I doubt it was financial.

More than likely, the move was an act of frustration in itself. By this time we had been meeting on Sundays for a little over two years, with attendance porpoising between fifty and sixty. You know your church is small when you can predict attendance within ten and mentally index for families on vacation.

The previous summer had been one of tremendous internal growth. We felt like our soul, mind, and expectations had exploded. Many in our congregation were experiencing similar things.

Sometime in this season—it's been years now so the order of things can get a little fuzzy—I had a dream that I suspected was from God. I use the word "suspected" because in that season, I wasn't quite sure how God spoke through dreams. I would have said I believed it was possible, but I had no personal experience of it, and I wasn't looking for any.

We had traveled to Pensacola, Florida, to visit the revival meetings that had so deeply impacted us before starting SpiritLife. While we were there, we made the standard Midwesterner's pilgrimage to the beach. You know the kind—where you drive there, get out, stare at the ocean, get in the car, and go back to where you came from. As I stood there on the sand, watching the waves roll in from the Gulf, I heard the Lord speak inwardly to me in a gentle way.

"How would you stop this?" He whispered.

I thought, "This is unstoppable. These waves just keep coming. Any wall you build at the shore—wood, concrete, whatever – would be smashed to bits in an hour."

That was it. There was no great follow up question, no point hammered home, but the thought was there. This is unstoppable. You'd better learn to live with it than to fight it.

That night, sleeping on a friend's futon, I dreamed again of the ocean. This time the waves were higher and stronger than they had been that day, and rather than viewing them from a distance, I was waist deep in the water. I could feel the rush of the sand over my feet and the tug of the sea. I braced myself as wave after wave shoved me to and fro until one finally broke my feet free of the sand. My body went parallel to the ocean floor and I was swept thirty or forty feet into the ocean by a retreating wave.

Just as I began to regain my footing, the outgoing wave was met by an incoming one and I was headed the other direction, only this time much faster and higher. The wave threatened to smash me onto the beach. I was terrified in the dream. I am not a strong swimmer—I would never have put myself in this position voluntarily. I remember screaming in the dream just as the wave receded and carried me back out to sea.

The dream may have only taken a moment in real time, but it seemed to repeat itself for hours. I would be swept out to sea, lifted on another wave, driven in toward the beach, scream out in fear, and be swept back out again. I woke up exhausted and, even if only in my imagination, a little sore.

I pondered the dream the entire day-long drive back to Cincinnati. I was particularly troubled because somehow, even through the fear and horror, I knew the waves were God. His question to me the day before, "How would you stop this?" was an illustration of His power. A few nights later, I had the same dream and spent the entire night getting beaten up in the ocean. Apparently, God was serious about this beat down. I was still trying to reconcile why it was happening to me and if this was a good thing or not. You find yourself on thin ice when wondering if a God thing is a good thing, but it was just that puzzling to me.

Later that week, I retold the two dreams to one of our board members. Congregations—particularly young ones—reflect the attitudes of their pastors. Chris was in the same camp as I was, believing that God could speak through a dream, but having pretty limited experience with it. He also had an incredibly tender ear toward the Lord. It was his dream to one day work in missions, but in this season he was working a desk job for a large corporation.

"What do you think it means?" he asked. Tears welled up in his eyes as he asked. He may not have known any more specifics than I did, but his spirit bore witness to the dream. When Jesus told us that His sheep know His voice, He didn't guarantee that they'd always know what He was saying. Even so, it was stirring to hear His voice, and we knew this was the voice of the Master.

This was the frustrating, "God, what are You saying?" situation that we were in when we moved from the apartment clubhouse to sharing the facility with the deaf church. Again, it was less strategic, and more feeling like we needed to change something because what we were doing was not working according to plan. I had read all the church planting books and by their timelines, we should have had several hundred in our congregation already. We had all the ingredients for success, including a budding move of the Holy Spirit. Surely the building was the problem.

The arrangement with the deaf church was that we would move our services to Sunday evenings. They used the building in the mornings and promised to leave it in pristine condition for us, as we would for them. Shortly after moving in, we began to understand that the word "pristine" has a range of interpretations. We assumed that they would pick up their bulletins, straighten chairs, and leave it ready for us to use. They, in turn, assumed "pristine" to mean they would leave.

At the very least, we would find stacks of bulletins everywhere, cold coffee in the coffee makers, and chairs askew. In their defense, they were a small congregation—smaller than ours. They were struggling with the debt of a large building. Our rent paid a significant part of the payment, but as renters, we could leave any time. Add to that mix the fact that they were a very conservative, deaf congregation, meaning we were culturally removed from them. Their pastor wore a tie to the office on Monday morning. I preached in jeans and boots and wore an earring. To be quite frank, I'm not sure the pastor was ever convinced he had rented the building to another church. He did cash the rent checks though.

The result of all this was that we found ourselves meeting on Sunday evenings rather than mornings, which felt at times like a setback to those of us with a traditional background. As a group, we were growing close, but as a church, we weren't growing. There is such a thing as growing pains, but there are also failure-to-grow pains which are much worse. They're an intricate mix of missed expectations, false hopes, and the fear that others are even more disappointed in you than you are.

From early on we enjoyed a sense of deep community. We had multifamily Dad and Kids Campouts in our backyard. I remember it getting colder than we thought it would—and the ground being harder than we hoped it would—which brought the multifamily campout into the house as a multifamily sleepover, only to discover the moms never left. I think five or six families spent the night. We all laughed about it in the morning over a huge pile of pancakes.

A large group of families rented a beach house for a week one summer. Each family took one night to cook, allowing the others to roam the beach all day. We came home deeply sunburned and deeply marked with appreciation for one another.

Our lives intersected at so many levels. Just entering our thirties, Kelsey and I were older than almost everyone in the church. Most of us had young children and were having more. Many of the guys in the church worked in the growing tech and business sectors of Cincinnati. We loved one another and loved Jesus together.

After we moved into the deaf church facility, we decided to do something traditional—something we'd never done before. We held a church potluck. It was a funny indicator of who we all were when we looked at the table laden with one or two pots of beans and eight variations of potatoes au gratin. It was clear what kind of church we were: very young marrieds with not a lot of cooking experience!

One Sunday, a family brought guests from their neighborhood. Newcomers were not an every week occurrence, so it was exciting for all of us. A church planter scrapping to make things work looks at every person they meet as a soul Jesus loves...and as someone who could bring real value to the church that God is building. The thought that God might add to our numbers was thrilling.

Later in the week, I made a phone call to the people who had brought the guests to get an idea of what their experience had been like. They told me, "Oh, they really liked it, but I'm not sure they'll be back..."

I couldn't quite figure out the logic in this, so I pressed a little harder. The response I got stopped me in my tracks.

"They said that our church was unique in that it really felt like a family."

I was encouraged by this—it certainly did have that feel. Then they continued, "Like a family they were not part of."

Ouch. I was face to face with my worst fear. I had hoped to help craft a body of believers with arms wide open to others, but under my direction it had turned inward. Again, this was not the fault of the body. People go where their leader leads them. I don't remember ever feeling frustrated toward the people. I do remember feeling a deep sense of disappointment in myself.

I would often spend part of Sunday afternoon in my basement office, praying and reading over my sermon notes. One Sunday, I sat on the couch in my office and realized that for the first time I was overwhelmingly tired. I muttered to myself, "I don't want to go." I hated to admit it, but it was true. I was tired of wondering why the church wouldn't grow, even though I loved God and the people dearly. I got down on the office floor and cried. It developed into crying out to God, but those first few minutes were just my own personal pain coming out. Hurting and crying out to God are slightly different things, and I had to go through the first to reach the second.

I repented for my disappointment, which even ten years later, I'm not sure is a sin. It felt like it at the time. In the midst of all that God was doing in our people, I was overwhelmingly disappointed that the church was not growing. In fact, through normal attrition such as people moving away, we were slowly getting smaller. People had been very kind, pretending not to notice, but it was hard not to miss a family when every family was so important.

I don't remember what I preached about that night. Given my state of mind, it's likely that many others don't remember it either. I do remember ending the service rather abruptly because I wanted it to be over. I wanted to get home where, perhaps for a moment, I would not be reminded that the church we'd hoped to build was not turning out like we had expected.

Later that week, I got a call from Chris. His phone calls were usually very encouraging to me. I say "usually" because as the treasurer, sometimes he had to deliver hard news, but even then he did it with grace. Chris was sent from the Lord for this season in our lives, I'm sure of it.

"Randy...I had your dream!"

The syntax of that statement threw me for a curve. I had no clue what he was talking about. The most intelligent answer I could come up with was, "Huh?"

"Your dream—the dream of the ocean? Getting smashed by the waves...I dreamed that!"

I felt cold chills cover my body. It was mind and spirit stretching for me at that point to consider that God would speak to someone in a dream to begin with, let alone give someone else the same dream.

I stammered, "You dreamed I was getting smashed in the ocean?"

"No, not exactly," he continued. "I was in your spot—getting lifted by the waves, pulled out to sea and getting hammered back onto the beach. I was terrified just like you were."

One would expect to find an element of solace in someone having a similar horrifying dream, but it just struck me as odd at the time. "Huh..." I answered. In retelling this story it is accentuated to me that I was probably never a very good pastor.

"And you were in the dream too, except..." his voice trailed off.

"Except what?" I pressed.

"Well, it's kind of odd..." he stammered.

"What? What's odd?" I asked. I wondered to myself if he'd seen me dead on the beach or half eaten by sharks.

"Well, as I was getting smashed onto the beach a couple of times, I saw you go by..."

"I'm alive! I'm still getting beaten to smithereens but I'm alive!" I thought. Then he continued.

"You were on...a surf board."

"Huh?"

"As I was being sucked back out to sea and lifted up, occassionally I would catch a glimpse of you," he explained. "You were on a surfboard."

I had no experience with prophetic dreams, so I was viewing all this with an eye of suspicion anyway, even if I had the original dream. Surely God was speaking somehow, but with me on a surfboard? Growing up in North Dakota, I rode anything that had wheels or legs. Motorcycles, horses, the occasional 4H steer...but I don't think I'd ever touched a surfboard in my life.

"A surfboard?" I asked.

"Yes, a surfboard. Even though I was petrified that I was going to get killed out there, I noticed and thought it was funny. It was like you'd been out there awhile and had figured out how to navigate the waves. They were killing you earlier, but now you looked like you were having fun."

"And you?" I wondered.

"They were still killing me!"

Chris's words about learning how to navigate the waves stuck with me. I thought about them constantly for the next few days. What on earth was God saying? Standing on the beach that day, I felt like the waves were the power of God. Their pounding me into the ground was not a theology I was comfortable developing. I liked the idea of the surfboard and wondered if it was possible to bypass my dream for his. I would soon learn that it was not.

I spent the next few months feeling like I was swept up in the first dream. I would be flooded with the presence of God in times of prayer, then walk into our own services and feel like I got pounded on the beach. Monday and Tuesday I'd be swept out to sea, hoisted into the air, and repeat the entire cycle by the end of the week. God was near, but He wasn't acting like I anticipated He would. The God that Sunday School had taught me was only gentle was playing rough and tumble with me. I didn't feel like a New Testament sheep—I felt more like Jacob wrestling an angel. In time, I would prevail, but my walk would certainly be different when I did.

We spend a great deal of time trying to reconcile our personal difficulties with our gross misunderstandings regarding God's sovereignty. Our belief in His sovereignty is valid and well placed. God is all powerful and works upon the elements of a man or woman's life. The breakdown happens when we project our own hopes, dreams, and assumptions onto His sovereign plan, essentially putting expectations on God that He would act like we would if we were given all the power in the world. This is where we encounter the truth that our thoughts are not like His thoughts and our ways are not like His ways.

People react in different ways to this realization. Some sink into deep depression as they come to terms with the fact that some of the dreams they've dreamed will not be realized. Others lift their eyes a little higher, trust in God's movement in their life, and determine for themselves that God is God and they are not. The first group is pounded on the beach as they fight soverignty. The second slowly learns what it means to ride the wave.

It took me in the neighborhood of a year to realize that I was taking a beating for a reason, and that there might be a different way to live. That's a long time to eat sand, but I'm a slow learner. Also, I knew that finally admitting that I saw what God was doing would mean changes that I was not sure I was able to bear.

In the next few months, two key events would take place that would mark my shifting from the first dream to the next. I didn't notice them as markers at the moment, but we rarely do.

Life-defining moments come to us as everyday occurrences, and only later do we comprehend the full weight of the matter. It's one more reason to delay self-evaluation until life experience has caught up.

SIXTEEN

Running Out of Changes
—∞—

All along this journey, I had increasingly enjoyed Steve Sjogren's friendship.

In some ways, we were unlikely friends. He was a movie and TV buff who had a massive big screen movie room in his basement. Our TV broke in our third year of marriage and we didn't replace it for nearly twenty years. He was open-minded in a California sort of way. I bordered on repressed. The paid staff of his church was twice the size of my congregation on a good Sunday.

That said, in other ways we were a natural fit. Two widely read introverts looking for someone to not have to talk to if we didn't want to. I remember Steve telling me once, "When I'm on an airplane and they're showing a movie, I pull out my laptop and watch my own movie. Sometimes it's the same movie, but I don't care." I laughed at him, but felt like I'd found an older brother.

We would sometimes talk several times a week, then a few weeks would pass without contact. When it resumed, it was usually in mid-sentence. This was back in the days before caller ID, so our phone would ring and I'd pick it up to hear him in mid-thought and I'd have to race to catch up. I raced a lot.

One Sunday while we were meeting in the clubhouse, I looked back to see Steve standing in the back. I was more than a little surprised—leaders of megachurches are generally fairly busy on Sunday mornings. When I glanced back a few minutes later, he was gone. That afternoon, the phone rang. In typical Steve fashion, there were no formalities.

"Hey, I was in your church today."

"Yes," I replied, "I saw you." It would have been hard to miss him.

"Yeah, and...the thing about your church is, it's kind of weird..."

I waited for the shoe to drop, but Steve could place a pause as accurately as he could choose words. The explanation did not automatically come. Finally, I broke the silence.

"Why is it weird, Steve?" I asked, and braced myself. Steve could be a very plain-spoken critic. What's worse, he wasn't often wrong, so I couldn't easily dismiss his observations.

"It's weird because your music is great, and your production is great, and your preaching is great. But nobody comes. That's just weird."

I felt like I was having a phone conversation with Captain Obvious. Nobody comes. Yes, that summarized things well. But it didn't help.

"So what's the answer?" I pressed.

"I don't know. It just seems like maybe you're not in the right place. Like you're wired for something different. I've gotta go." And with that, the conversation was over, but flames of "What on earth am I doing" were fanned like never before.

Through our association with Steve, we were introduced to a number of his church staff. One favorite was Rusty Geverdt, who directed the prayer ministry that took place after each service, as well as a number of other initiatives. Rusty had a quiet but prophetic way about him that led people to lean into what he was saying for fear of missing a word. He didn't say a lot of words, but the ones he did carried great weight.

On the side, Rusty helped lead a prayer meeting with a group from multiple churches. Like SpiritLife's Saturday evening meetings, it melded Scripture, prayer, and worship in a way that made prayer doable and time fly. Eventually we joined our Saturday meeting with theirs, and enjoyed doing in a larger group what we had stumbled toward as a small one.

Kelsey, in particular, found her place in this group and led many of the meetings. I took a back seat and helped in the tech booth with visuals.

I enjoyed seeing her get her chance and watching how Rusty honored and regarded her. I often joke that I am the last one on the bus in our relationship—that Kelsey often senses a direction before I do. That said, once I am on the bus, I can assure you we are going there, wherever "there" is. In a very real way, Kelsey got on this prayer bus early and patiently waited for me.

I wasn't resistant toward the prayer element. Neither was I experienced in it. I saw the value and certainly had a private prayer time, but gathering with a group always wore me out. Like Steve, I was happier "watching my own movie." Every Saturday we met in the Vineyard Resource Center, an administrative building on the Vineyard campus that had a meeting space for about 100 people comfortably. We'd put 125 in it some nights. I was always touched to see so many people from so many different traditions come together around Scripture and music to find their unified voice in prayer. As difficult as it was to put my hand toward Sunday night church services, it was easy to come on Saturday night and join the others in prayer.

Noting that we were struggling with our Sunday night SpiritLife meeting, Steve suggested we move our services to the VRC on Sunday morning. The idea of meeting on the same property as another church might seem odd to some, but the Cincinnati Vineyard has enjoyed a long history of generosity and open-handedness. Leaders welcomed us with open arms and even loaned us musicians on Sundays when we needed them.

Landing at the VRC for Sunday morning services made life a little easier. It certainly eased our strained church budget, as the Vineyard charged us no rent. Our setup was much easier and the smaller room had a much warmer feel than the cold, stark auditorium that we had been using.

Moving our church to Vineyard property also made the lines between myself and the Vineyard a little more blurry. I was invited to join their staff meetings for trainings. After several years of working on things with a very small team, I appreciated the camaraderie and certainly needed the seasoned input into my leadership style.

We coordinated outreach efforts with The Vineyard and found them generous in their lending of whatever they had that we needed. One Halloween they loaned us an ice cream truck that had been heavily modified with low rider hydraulics. There is nothing as fun as passing candy out of an ice cream truck that's shaking violently.

The growing relationships—both within The Vineyard and with the growing prayer community—made the VRC a home of sorts that we'd never had. For the first time in a long time, Kelsey and I felt connected to something bigger than us. We had long been a part of our denomination, but during the church plant years had gone down a different path culturally. Our jeans and t-shirts, my earrings, our church's propensity to take a break for bagels midway through the service, all made The Vineyard world feel more normal than the world we were from.

About this time we began hearing about a prayer movement in Kansas City, Missouri, directed by Mike Bickle. Kelsey had never heard of him, but I vaguely remembered reading an article about him when I was in college. The prayer model being used by the prayer group we were part of—the Cincinnati House of Prayer, as it had taken to referring to itself as—was based on a model developed at Kansas City's International House of Prayer.

Dear friends of ours from our Tennessee days had gone to IHOP-KC for a conference and told us, "You really need to check this out."

I'm not sure how it was decided that I should attend alone. I'm sure it was a matter of childcare and finances, but I have never really enjoyed conferences, so it was highly uncharacteristic of me to go alone.

I flew to Kansas City, navigated a shuttle to the hotel, and found my room. I remember registering for the conference, and being a little surprised to see nearly the entire operation being run by young people. By young, I mean 17-22 year olds. They were everywhere. The meeting had a bit of the chaos expected with a gathering run by young people, but it added to the excitement. I was unsure what to expect.

In that first meeting, I heard Mike preach what he would call a forerunner message. It was the life story and mission of John the Baptist, and it was not Western Christianity 101. He preached prayer, fasting, sacrifice, radical commitment, generosity, and the power to conquer fear in pursuit of God's best. He preached with conviction that only comes from knowing the subject firsthand. Mike had lived far below his means for thirty years, voluntarily limiting his income from books and audio recordings as a statement before the Lord of His commitment to fasting not only food but the things that distract so many from their calling. As he closed his message and asked people to commit to a John the Baptist lifestyle, he wasn't asking them to move to the desert or eat bugs. He was asking them to wholeheartedly pursue God at any cost, even to the point of being considered an outsider in their own culture.

Hundreds of people flooded the aisles and walked toward the front of the hotel ballroom as a public statement of their commitment. I stood, made my way to the aisle, and went the opposite direction—down the hall, up the elevator, to my room. I knew that God was doing something in me, but I had to talk to Kelsey.

It was late afternoon in Cincinnati when Kelsey answered the phone. I could hear the roar of a house full of boys in the background when she picked up the receiver.

"Hey, Honey!" she answered, "Aren't you in a conference session?" I was not known for attending conferences, and when I did attend, I was notorious for skipping the sessions.

"I just got out," I assured her.

"How was it?" she asked, excitedly. She was very interested in what was happening in Kansas City's prayer room.

"This guy is preaching our message, Kelsey," I said. "It's prayer, fasting, John the Baptist revolution stuff...but it's different."

"What's different?" she wondered.

"He knows what he's talking about."

I had clearly been led by the Lord to preach what we'd been preaching, but for the first time I had to admit that I was a lot of smoke, but little fire. It doesn't mean the smoke wasn't genuine or that I didn't want to generate fire, but I simply didn't have the life experience that Bickle had. I was talking myself into something that he had been living for decades, and I was fascinated.

Mike's style was not mine. I was understated and conversational. He was loud. I was painfully conscious of my language and bringing others into understanding what I was saying. He had an unusual vocabulary, chock full of phrases that, while biblical, were difficult for newcomers to track with. His organization had made do by simplifying many of their programs and initiatives into three letter acronyms. It was so pervasive that years later, IHOP staffer Derek Loux would record his infamous "Acronym Song," stringing together all of them into a hilarious, indecipherable package.

Style aside, Mike's message rang true. The revolution he was calling for started within. Historically, when words like "revolution" were thrown around, they were accompanied by demands to be placed on leaders. When this army of young people cried out for change, they were asking God to help change themselves. They saw themselves as much a part of the problem as the solution, and they saw God as a loving Father who was there to help them sort the good from the bad.

I went back to the evening session and was treated to much of the same. It was as if I was watching the natural progression of what God had been speaking to us from the very early planting days, telescoped out decades and projected on a big stage. It was challenging, but even so it was affirming to think that we were hearing God. We weren't crazy. We may have been inexperienced, but we were onto something.

In the months to follow, Kelsey and I made a number of trips to similar conferences. Sometimes we'd go together, other times we would travel alone. We always brought home CDs and cassettes with Bickle's unique admonition, "My copyright is your right to copy, so have at it." What The Vineyard was with grace, giving it freely and widely, Bickle was with content and encouragement.

Bickle and Sjogren were different as night and day in some ways and surprisingly similar in others. Both enjoyed poking fun at themselves and their efforts. Early in his church planting days, Steve would invite people to come to his church "maybe in a year or so, when we get better." Mike often referred to the International House of Prayer as "little, rough and ugly," and lowered expectations by insisting that they were building a ship at sea. None of this had much effect on how we felt about what we were hearing.

As Sjogren had made evangelism and outreach doable, Bickle was making prayer accessible to people with the Harp and Bowl model developed under his tutelage.

We began to drink deeply from this stream of teaching that called us to a higher standard of holiness, but also showed us a depth of love in God that we had personally not explored. Even as we were being affected, we were being encouraged. God had not been silent these past few years. Every time I'd been picked up and smashed on the rocks by the waves of what He was doing, I was being tenderized.

One of my many errors in church planting was in present-ing the church as the center of life. I'm not sure if I ever actually verbalized this, but in my mind, the local body had its own heart, its own unique circulatory system, its own nervous system that any believer could tap into for purposes of revitalization.

That perspective is not without merit, but when planting a church thinking that way, I often found myself trying to convince people to commit to an entity that would do for them what they might not be able to do for themselves. At the same time, I was relying on them to help get the entity to the point where it could help others. It's like the old joke about the small town voting to build a new jail. They decide it would be most cost effective to use building supplies scavenged from the destruction of the old jail, but they vow to use the old jail until the new jail is complete. I stretched immediately to build a body when I should have started with building people. If I have one regret from our years at Spir-itLife, it lies in worrying too much about the whole and too little about the parts.

I meant well, but wish I had spent more time exploring the individual needs of our leaders and helping meet them. In retro-spect, I can understand if people felt I was looking past them even as I shook their hand. It wasn't that they weren't important or dear to me. I simply did not understand the upside-down nature of the kingdom of God, or have the basic leadership skills that would have told me to take better care of my leaders. To their credit, they never grew angry or disillusioned, or if they did, they were so godly that I wasn't able to perceive it. I do feel, however, that I was given a group of young eagles and the kingdom of God would have been better served if I had concentrated on making them strong, rather than worrying how many other eagles were out there.

Distance in space and time do wonders for our perspective. It's often far easier to see clearly at a distance than it is up close, especially when looking backward. Literally, as I write this portion

I'm gaining understanding about what God was doing through the struggle of our church plant.

At the time, my motives were pure, even if my tactics were skewed. Even now I can see how God was pleased by all we were doing, but it's the kind of pleased that I feel myself when I watch my children build sand castles. I love that they're trying and I know that it's important to their development, but I'm not terribly worried about the castle surviving. The true value is in the doing, not the having. God was not building a local church body, He was allowing us to interact with these people and learn who we are so that we would later focus on what we were fully called to do.

Today, roughly a decade later, I'm grateful for what we learned during that whole time. In the moment, however, I was miserable. I wasn't angry with anyone. I couldn't figure out who to be angry with. I was disappointed in myself. I was disappointed with circumstances, because I expected them to be so different a few years into a church plant. In spite of all we thought would happen, we found ourselves three years old as a church, no bigger than we were on day one, in a borrowed facility, in a sort of economic life support through the benevolence of The Vineyard who allowed us to meet there. We still had, as Steve pointed out, good music and good teaching, but some Sundays it felt like playing church. Not in a pretend way, but like an eight year old might mimic his dad's preaching. Sincere, but hardly sustainable or life-changing.

During the previous three years, we had changed a lot of things. We'd changed locations every few months. We'd changed our service times and our service order. We changed how we thought about small groups and where we spent our outreach funds. For a small church, we were running out of things to change.

SEVENTEEN

Plant or Die Trying

—ɯ—

Even as we were enjoying our exploration into the prayer movement, participating more and more in the Saturday evening prayer
meetings, we were puzzled with what to do regarding SpiritLife.
For a season, it felt like we'd gone into slow motion, with little
happening during the week between our small services. To be fair,
nearly every family in the congregation had added to their family
in the previous two years, in some cases more than one child. We
were growing families, but we weren't growing as a body and it
had become painfully awkward for me to face.

In a board discussion about the overall situation, one board
member said, "Healthy things grow..." He wasn't complaining. He
was puzzled—because I know he loved us and loved the people in
the church. Nevertheless, that comment stuck with me. Healthy
things grow...and this isn't growing. What could the fix be?

We had been blessed by the hard work of Adam and Melody,
who had moved with us from Tennessee to lead worship. They had
every bit as much energy and emotional investment in SpiritLife as
Kelsey and I did. During the years we were planting, they received
a salary so small that it's not even worth mentioning—if I had to

guess, we might have paid Adam roughly what he spent in guitar string replacement. They clearly served for the love of the mission, because there wasn't much else in it for them.

In spite of the difficulties we faced, our relationship stayed strong. Through the leanest of times, I can only remember once or twice where frustration arose, and each time it was resolved in a day or two. They were godly, consistent, and a pleasure to work with.

Some months after moving our services to the VRC, Adam and Melody asked to meet with Kelsey and I. We knew they had something big to discuss. The sort of friends who walk into your house without knocking are not given to asking for a meeting unless it's important. In that meeting, they explained how they'd felt for some time that the Lord might be leading them to step down. Adam had been offered a role in Student Ministries at The Vineyard, and they planned to transition in a month to six weeks.

It would be wrong to say that it wasn't discouraging, but it was certainly understandable. The plan was for SpiritLife to help support them as soon as possible after we launched. Now, three years later, we were arguably further from that point than before. Adam and Melody had both worked second and third jobs to make ends meet. They had such excellent spirits that I can honestly say I never heard either of them complain about unfulfilled promises. They just put their hands to the plow.

Adam's side jobs had given him access to a lot of production equipment. He'd spent a lot of time working after hours and learning how to produce audio and video and now had a bevy of skills that The Vineyard needed. I should also say that there was no frustration with The Vineyard about "hiring people away." In some ways, I was relieved for them. They were going to be able to pay their bills—or at least nearly pay their bills—doing what they loved to do. It seemed as much like the Lord's hand to me as it did to them. We prayed for them and blessed them in this endeavor.

Adam helped transition us to another worship leader and joined The Vineyard staff.

It was, in my own heart, a sort of release. I was not pleased that they were gone, because we missed them greatly, but in a sense it opened the door to the obvious. SpiritLife was not panning out as we expected. Up until this point, it felt important to pretend that things were going to turn around soon. Perhaps this week we'd be flooded with guests. Perhaps the next week everything would be different.

Their departure forced me to admit to myself that perhaps SpiritLife was not going to be the next Saddleback or the next Vineyard. In fact, it might never amount to much at all. Instinctively, I think I knew we had turned a corner—not because of their leaving, but marked by their leaving.

Sometimes, you remember the exact genesis of a thought. Then, there are some processes that are so all-encompassing that it is hard to find the edges. I remember a lot of specifics about those days, but I do not remember first entertaining the idea that perhaps I was part of the problem SpiritLife was experiencing. I'm sure I thought about it a long time. I argued with myself. I didn't want to be a quitter, but I was already struggling with feeling like a failure. It didn't seem to be fair that those were the only two options I had to choose from.

At some point, I broached the subject with Kelsey. "We've changed everything and the church is not growing. At least, we've changed everything but us."

As I've mentioned before, Kelsey has always had a larger prophetic sail than I do. I have rarely stumbled into something that I was sensing from the Lord that she didn't already have better developed thoughts and language for. It's a gift and meant that she was not surprised by this line of thinking.

All the while, I grew closer to some of the staff at The Vineyard. One day, I was asked if I'd consider a role in youth ministry. I had enjoyed youth pastoring in Tennessee, and here was an opportunity to do it on a larger scale. It involved leading the team that ministered to the several hundred teens who gathered every week. I was asked to speak to them one weekend and it seemed to go well.

Kelsey and I explored the role at great length and once it was officially offered, even decided we would take it. We were asked to meet with leaders at The Vineyard to finalize things like job description details and salary. On the twenty minute drive from our home to the church, one of us—I'm not even sure who—confessed that something didn't feel right about this. We didn't have misgivings about considering other things, but this particular role was not what God had planned. By the time we parked our car in The Vineyard parking lot, we both agreed that we would in all likelihood not take the role. Fifteen minutes into the meeting, I knew we were right and had to say, "Thank you, but no thank you."

I was a little mystified really, even though I'd been the one who threw the brakes on it. Transitioning to The Vineyard felt very natural, but the door seemed closed. I was confused because I felt I'd heard from God.

Six weeks later, God called back—or rather, The Vineyard did. There was another role open. They wondered if I would be interested. After a few days of prayer and some long discussions, Kelsey and I agreed this was the Lord's hand. It was decided. I would resign from SpiritLife. It felt like resignation in every sense of the word.

It's said that most pastors resign every Monday morning and then tear up the resignation before someone finds it. That was never my situation. I loved SpiritLife, adored the people who labored alongside us, and had moved to Cincinnati to plant a church or die trying. I didn't realize the dying would be metaphorical. In some ways, I was less prepared for that. Martyrdom has a certain glory to it and ends with a bang. This wasn't the way I wanted to go out.

Sunday morning, I asked the board and their wives to meet me for a few minutes after the service. After the last amen was said and the room was cleaned up, we all filed into a small classroom and sat on folding chairs. I could tell by the way they looked at each other that they were curious, but not particularly concerned. The nature of a small church is that decisions are often made on the fly, and we had often met as couples, so there was nothing extremely out of the ordinary about this meeting...except that there was.

The moment I began to speak, they sobered. I spoke about how I had been praying about the direction of the church and that I'd come to the realization that we had to put everything up for discussion. I explained that in that line of thought, I'd realized that it was time for me to step down as the pastor.

They had questions—nothing hurtful, just questions on the process, what this meant for us and what it meant for them. They did not go into this thinking they would lead a church, and I did not present it to them originally as something that would land in their lap. There were a lot of changes coming—as many for them as for me.

We did not meet long, perhaps fifteen minutes at the most. I don't remember much of what was said. I do remember seeing tears in people's eyes. I remember it being extremely awkward. I remember a dual sense of having a weight off my shoulders but overwhelming sadness. I also remember walking out alone, perhaps ten feet ahead of the others, but feeling very far away. Kelsey and I got in our van and quietly drove home. Our dream had died and we knew it.

I gave the leadership of the church six weeks advance notice. Protocol for ministers is to give a month, but I wanted them to have more than that. I'll confess, those were a long six weeks—not because anyone was angry or hateful, but because they were remarkably quiet. There were a few vague side conversations about changing seasons and God's will, but there were no sit down, heart-to-heart conversations about how anyone was doing. Monday through Saturday activity of the church essentially ceased and we simply did a Sunday service that felt somehow like an extended funeral.

In the moment, I was a little hurt over the silence from others, but time brings perspective, and I realize now that I caused any difficulty that took place. After having led them on a three year journey that spoke grandly about the future, I took a hard left turn and expected them to continue on as if it had been part of the plan. It was not that they questioned that I had heard from the Lord—at least publicly, they were all supportive—but I had done nothing to bring them along in the decision making process. Once I began thinking about resigning, I closed ranks and held those conversations only between Kelsey, the Lord, and me. Although unintended, I can see how that could have been interpreted as a lack of trust on my part. We had gone through a lot together—children being born, parents dying, financial crises, all the things life is made of—and in a decision that affected us all, I had closed ranks and made the call without considering them.

No doubt adding to the difficulty was the fact that I was moving to a role in a large church within sight of where our small church was meeting. That's no exaggeration—we were meeting on Vineyard property. The main building was only a couple of hundred feet away. To the SpiritLife congregation, it probably felt like I was leaving them in the log cabin and walking away to a new suite at the Ritz Carlton. Again, no one ever verbalized that, but it's likely that it felt like that because it certainly looked like that.

The primary question about SpiritLife's survival lay in answering who would become the pastor. We were under certain guidelines as part of our denomination, but I also knew that we were viewed as a bit of a one-off. My fear was that a pastor would be appointed in a reactionary manner, perhaps to counter the offbeat angle that SpiritLife approached things from under my leadership. Before I called the denomination to tell them of my situation, I placed another call to a friend who was looking for a pastorate. He was of excellent reputation, was far more pastoral than I was, and had spoken at SpiritLife a number of times. As a known quantity, I had confidence that the congregation would follow his leadership as smoothly as possible. I explained to him that we were leaving and I wanted him to consider becoming the pastor. It should be noted that this is not how these sorts of things are done in this particular denomination, but I was beyond adhering to conventional wisdom at this point. I desperately loved these people, wanted the best for them, and believed this was the best.

After a number of long conversations, he agreed that this might be a good fit for his family and the church. With that, I called the denominational office and within a ten minute conversation, presented them with a problem, namely that one of their more unusual churches was about to be without a pastor, and a solution to that problem in the form of a minister whom they already had great faith, who was without a church and willing to take the role. They said they'd get back to us. Within a few days, they gave it their stamp of approval.

When I presented the idea to the church board, they were uniformly positive about it. Driving home from that meeting, a sense of peace flooded over me that I had not felt in a long time. The only thing I might compare it to is what someone must feel like once they've made an adoption plan for their child. There is a sense of loss, but also a gratefulness because that which is so important to them will now be cared for.

A few months earlier, when I'd started thinking about resigning from the church, I had a series of six vivid dreams. I rarely dream, and when I do, I don't remember much of it, but for several weeks, every few days I would dream in full technicolor with the surround sound turned on high. I would wake up and write the dreams down. They were all so real and yet so unlikely.

In the first dream, a Vineyard staff member who I knew quite well was sitting across the table from me in a Macaroni Grill restaurant. He was explaining to me in detail what his duties were because I was going to inherit them. I told Kelsey about the dream but never mentioned it to another soul. The other five dreams came just as randomly. They were vivid, but defied explanation and resisted any sort of attempt to establish common ground between them.

I hit the ground running with my role at The Vineyard. The role I ultimately filled was a great fit, allowing for a lot of creativity and working with people I really enjoyed. At that time, the church was structured around five pillars. My role fell into the Evangelism pillar, which unbeknown to me had undergone a lot of turnover in the months prior to my joining. After a few weeks of finding my place, I was invited to attend a restructuring meeting. At the time, I'm not sure that I even knew what that meant.

Given the high percentage of new people on the team, it was clear that we needed some sort of hierarchy. After talking about roles and skills for a few hours, a decision was made and I suddenly had about a half dozen people reporting to me. Keep in mind, I'd never really had a paid employee in my life. I nearly panicked when I realized that Monday morning, all of those people were going to be looking to me for direction. Fortunately, they were all highly skilled and motivated, allowing me to pretend to be the boss until I figured out how to be the boss.

This all took place during the original dot com boom, when wacky titles were all the rage in startup companies. As my role developed, there was a lot of conversation about what exactly my job title would be. Most of what was proposed sounded insanely boring.

The church had been founded on Servant Evangelism, and embossed in gigantic letters on the outside of the building was the phrase: "Small Things Done With Great Love Will Change the World." One morning I pulled up to the building, saw those letters for the umpteenth time, and decided on my title. From that day forward, in print, in person and on the web, I was referred to as the Director of Small Things.

A few days after the restructuring meeting, a co-worker asked if I wanted to grab lunch. I looked forward to getting to know him better, so I eagerly agreed. We drove a half mile to a Macaroni Grill where we were shown to a table...the exact table I'd dreamed of a few months earlier. In fact, not only was it the same table, but it was the same staff member from my dream. Chills ran up my spine. I'd never had something happen like this. Then, he started in on why he'd asked me to grab lunch. He had been contemplating a ministry move and decided that now was the time. He would be taking a role with the Dayton Vineyard, and due to my leadership role at VCC, his duties would fall primarily into my basket. He then proceeded to explain what each of those duties was. My dream was happening, right down to sitting at the same table.

Over the next few weeks, four more dreams came to fruition exactly as I dreamed them. None of them were earthshaking as a stand alone event, but they each were a unique signpost to me that God was speaking to us in a new way that I could rely on—that when I sensed a dream was from God, it was really from God. On a side note, the sixth dream remains very personal and as of this writing, unrealized. I believe for it though, knowing that God completes what He puts His hand to.

Even as I was watching dreams come to fruition, there was the dream of the church plant that was on life-support. The new pastor and his wife did a great job of regrouping the congregation and laying out plans to go forward. The church embraced his leadership, and even though the immediate situation did not change, there was hope. I knew we had made a good choice.

A few months after I'd made my transition, I received a phone call from the pastor. I was excited to hear from him—he and his wife had become dear friends of ours. I could tell three seconds into the phone call, however, that this was not necessarily good news.

"They've closed the church, Randy," he said.

I couldn't quite comprehend what he was saying or who "they" were. "What?" I stammered.

"SpiritLife. The denomination called. They want us to close the doors in two weeks."

I couldn't believe what I was hearing. The church was certainly not successful as some would term it, but neither was it a drag on resources. It had received some money at its inception but had been self-sufficient for the past two years. It was costing nothing, even if it was struggling along. I knew of a dozen churches locally that they were supporting financially, yet continued to allow to exist. I have no explanation for their decision and have wondered for years exactly why things transpired the way they did.

I hung up the phone and swallowed hard. SpiritLife was over.

EIGHTEEN

Santa is Drunk

—ɯ—

SpiritLife's sudden closing was a shock. I resigned believing that it was a last ditch effort for its survival, and for it to close made me wonder if I'd waited too long. Perhaps I should have resigned a year earlier.

Up until this point I'd been struggling with the realization that I'd failed to build the vibrant church I imagined. Now I faced the additional weight of wondering if I was responsible for its demise. I was perplexed by the denomination's decision, but felt like I had little room to question it. It would have been a little like complaining that the game was called off after you'd already announced you were quitting. I felt especially bad for those who had been left, including the pastor. I had presented the opportunity with such hope for the future. I felt like I'd sold someone a used car, only to watch the motor blow as he drove away.

I dealt with the pain by throwing myself into my new role.

In any new role there is a season of getting up to speed. For me, at The Vineyard, there was getting up to speed and getting up to scale. Understand that when it comes to a congregation, bigger is not always better. It is certainly often different, and going from 60 people to 6,000 people was an eye opener.

Later I would liken it to going from riding a dirt bike to riding a superbike on a speedway. I grew up riding dirt bikes. It is very physical and takes more brute force than finesse. You can launch a dirt bike off a jump and manipulate it mid-air to land slightly to one side or another. It is a forgiving, inexact activity. Church planting was like that—one might have an idea on Thursday and execute it that weekend. The Vineyard was like riding on a speedway at 170 miles an hour—one could go very, very fast, but it took planning and care. If you tilted your head for a moment to look to the side, it might have very unintended repercussions.

At SpiritLife, we could literally change locations of the church midweek—it was a matter of making some phone calls. At The Vineyard, changing the smallest detail had to be thought through completely because it involved so many other people and teams. It was an area of training that I desperately needed.

In addition to the complexity of the church, I was surprised at all of the offbeat things that would happen. SpiritLife was hard to find. This was a curse at times, but a blessing at others. The Vineyard was high profile. If you moved to town and were looking for a church, someone was likely to invite you. Likewise, if you woke up one morning thinking, "I'm going to church to do something completely nuts," you probably ended up at The Vineyard as well.

The first event that I had leadership over was the annual Christmas Eve outreach. A primary value at The Vineyard was being outward-focused. The church constantly looked to reach people where they were as opposed to bringing them into a building to find God. We looked at Christmas Eve as an opportunity to extend the love of God. With donuts.

Early on the morning of December 24th, I drove north of Cincinnati with a box truck. About halfway between Cincinnati and Dayton, I exited I-75 and drove on a back road several miles to find the Holy Grail of Confectionary Goodness: the Krispy Kreme factory. There, I backed up and they loaded one thousand dozen donuts into the truck.

Once back at The Vineyard, my team taped directions and a map to each box of Krispy Kremes and then divided them into different sectors in the city. Each map marked a fire station, a nursing home, a convenience store—someplace where someone would be working on Christmas Eve. The instructions were to deliver donuts and offer to pray for people.

The service was scheduled to start at 4:30 p.m. I remember a long debate over the starting time—it seemed too insanely early for my train of thought. I lost the debate, though, and at 4:20 p.m. I walked into the auditorium from a side door and found each of the 2,200 seats full. We were standing room only—perhaps 2,500 people. I had two immediate thoughts. First, God is awesome. Second, I do not have enough donuts. Who would think one would ever need more than a thousand dozen of anything?

We did a lot of things well at The Vineyard. Reverence was not one of them. It was a fun atmosphere and sobriety was not one of our strong suits. Nevertheless, each year during the Christmas Eve service, we gave it a try with Christmas carols on acoustic guitars and a candlelit service. We were about halfway through the first song when I noticed Santa Claus walking down the aisle, greeting people as if he were running for office.

At the time, I remember thinking, "This is strange...even for The Vineyard." but I didn't really think much more about it, until my walkie-talkie crackled with the voice of someone from the hospitality team.

"Hey everyone, whose Santa Claus is that?"

Silence.

"Facilities, is he yours?" they asked.

After a moment, the answer came, "No...he's not ours."

The next question was, "Randy? Is this your Santa?"

I assured them that he wasn't my Santa. This all became very strange as we wondered how Santa, who one would assume to be very busy on Christmas Eve, would have time to wander the aisles of The Vineyard. An usher quietly walked down, gently grabbed

him by the elbow and asked him if he would wait in the foyer to
talk with people, as it was a little distracting to have him wandering around during the service. Mr. Claus, gracious by nature,
obliged. He walked out the back of the auditorium and I assumed
the episode was over.

A few minutes later, as candles began to be lit across the congregation, the radio silence broke. "Santa is in the balcony. Repeat,
Santa is in the balcony." I looked up to see him near the railing,
holding a laughing two year old and surrounded by children. Then
the person on the radio continued.

"And he's drunk. He's very drunk."

With Secret Service precision, the facilities swept in on Old
Saint Nick from two sides and walked him out. Parents, unaware
of Santa's inebriated state, were a little upset because they were
hoping he would talk to the kids. For his part, Santa started speaking loudly on his way out, promising kids all sorts of gifts by the
next morning. At one point he assured a child, "You'll get that
pony you want tomorrow!" Parents were left wondering how they
were going to deliver on Santa's promises.

Santa spent the rest of the service in a back office nursing a
cup of black coffee. This sort of thing happened at The Vineyard.
It was a whole new world for me though.

My title of Director of Small Things was remarkable in that it
was hard for anyone to actually pin down what my job was. I had
a job description, but even it was a little vague. I was responsible
for outreach, but what that looked like was largely up to me. I held
close to Sjogren's values of kindness outreach, sending hundreds
of volunteers out each Saturday to give away bottles of water, wash
windshields, and clean toilets in businesses as a way to show the
love of God in a practical way.

I also gave direction to The Vineyard's successful Alpha program, teaching Bible basics to several hundred people at a time.
Often the majority were unbelievers who would politely listen in
silence as I talked about the value of Scripture or the basics of

prayer, only to tell their small group leaders, "He's nuts—that can't be true." Through good small group leadership, many of them would come to faith during the eight weeks of Alpha.

Near the end of Alpha, the entire group does a one day retreat that explores the role of the Holy Spirit in the life of a Christian. Most attendees approach this with a bit of apprehension. These are the same people who were questioning the importance of prayer seven weeks earlier, so the idea of the Spirit living within them is quite a stretch for them. I was team teaching the day with Rusty, our friend from the Saturday evening prayer meetings. Rusty had a gift for making the things of the Spirit less spooky than most. These events were always hugely successful, with the Holy Spirit touching many people at a deep level.

Preparing for one of the Alpha retreats with Rusty, we discussed who to ask to lead worship and he suggested Julie, the wife of one of our SpiritLife board members. I readily agreed—Julie and her husband, Mark, were very dear to us and had gone out of their way to encourage us through all this. Nevertheless, when the day came, it did feel a little strange to be ministering together again. We sat on the front row of the conference room together and I quipped to her, "Here we are again...rented chairs and a portable sound system."

Julie laughed and said, "Those were all good times, Randy."

I must have shot her an odd look, because she immediately asked, "Do you feel strangely about all that?"

"Strangely" was an understatement. "Julie, I feel awful," I admitted.

She seemed astonished. "Why, Randy? I don't understand?"

"Julie, I feel like I wasted a lot of people's time and money. Everyone worked so hard—you guys worked so hard—and now, it's done." My emotions were split—part of me did not want to have this conversation and part of me craved it.

Her eyes grew big. What I felt was so obvious to everyone was a new thought to her. "Randy...that time and those dollars were not wasted. What God did in that season is not negated by us not having church services now...that was all real. We do not feel any of what you are feeling in regard to regret. We look at that as a rich time."

Although it didn't entirely assuage my feelings, that conversation was one of the kindest discussions I'd ever had. I wasn't even convinced that everyone felt like Julie did—just to know that someone did meant the world to me. Maybe not all of that effort had gone up in smoke. Maybe good had been done, even amid the pain.

After a few months, I was also asked to give leadership to VCC's church planting internship. I saw this invitation coming because it made good sense on the org chart, but the irony of directing church planters and church planting after our church plant failed was almost more than I could take.

We had three couples who were looking to plant churches in the next year. My role was to walk them through their plans, coach them, and cheer them on to victory. We would meet each Saturday morning over coffee and donuts to discuss how they were doing and address areas of concern. The first weekend, I sat them down and told them my whole story...that some years ago, I was in a meeting just like this, fighting for the values of the church that God was birthing within me, and that after years of long hard work, the church failed. It was not the fiery coaching speech they anticipated. That said, it was probably the most realistic thing I could have told them.

As I poured myself into my role at The Vineyard, Kelsey became more and more involved in the prayer ministry on Saturday nights. The group expanded in influence and hours. Her heart came alive in those settings.

Periodically we would sneak out to Kansas City for conferences at the International House of Prayer. The message of intimacy with Jesus was like water to our soul and also helped us envision exactly how the Lord felt about us, whether the church we had planted was thriving or dead. Personally, I began to see for the first time how performance-minded I expected God to be.

Eventually the Cincinnati House of Prayer hosted a conference at The Vineyard and brought IHOP-KC speakers and musicians. As a bridge between the church and the prayer effort, I did airport runs and hung out in the green room, where I met Aaron Walsh. In his mid-twenties, Aaron was scheduled to be one of the speakers. I'll confess now—I was concerned. I remember what I preached like in my mid-twenties, and the thought of sitting through a conference's worth of that made me want to lay down in a dark room.

When Aaron got up to preach, however, my attitude changed. In humility, and very aware of his youth, he spoke with an authority that is rarely seen even in a forty year old. Session after session, he preached on the love of the Father and the knowledge of God. I would sit in the back row bewildered, wondering how someone as young as this could speak with this depth.

During breaks, Aaron and I would sit in the green room, where I would pester him with questions about IHOP-KC. He would do the same to me regarding doing church with thousands of people. Finally I asked, "How did you get to preach like you do when you're so young?"

He laughed and said, "You should have seen me a few years ago. In my late teens, I was a drunk."

"Really?" I asked. I remember thinking that a lot of things must have happened in a few years. I pressed him, "What changed?"

"The prayer room," he replied.

With that, I began watching the rest of the crew from IHOP-KC. They were almost all as young as Aaron or younger, and while they were clearly still young adults, they talked of the things of the Lord in a way that few people I knew did. It was firsthand, experiential knowledge that only comes with extended times with Jesus. These might have been kids, but they had a lot to teach me about God's nature and how to communicate with Him.

Before the conference ended, Aaron asked me, "Would you ever consider moving to Kansas City to be part of the House of Prayer?"

I didn't answer him—not because I hadn't been thinking about it, but because I couldn't imagine leaving my role at The Vineyard. It was too healing after being beaten up by church planting. I wasn't so sure I wanted to build another house on a peninsula again. Little did I know that we were about to be called further out onto the point than we ever expected.

A few months after the conference, Aaron called me. He asked if I'd come out to IHOP-KC to talk with Mike Bickle about out-reach in a prayer context. It seemed like a fascinating conversation, so Kelsey and I made plans to visit. Aaron made it clear from the start that he thought we would move there, but personally, I was not convinced.

We drove to Kansas City excited about meeting with Mike. We had listened to his preaching for several years now, and appreciated the depth of his insight into Scripture and practical application for the believer. What we didn't anticipate was his down-to-earth nature. Sitting down around a small table in the coffee shop adjacent to the prayer room, Mike asked us fifty questions about what we'd done and what was on our hearts. It didn't feel like an interview – and for all practical purposes, it wasn't. It just felt like someone who was interested in who we were. Later we would learn of Mike's insatiable curiosity about people.

After hearing our story, he told us an abbreviated version of how the House of Prayer got started and why it was important. Then, in his typical low key fashion, he explained the leadership structure of the organization, describing it at various points as "little, rough and ugly," "the beginning of the beginning," and repeatedly, as "dorky." He was clear that nothing was set in stone at IHOP-KC, that roles changed regularly, and that the only rea-son to move there would be the prayer room. Then he dropped the bomb.

"I want you to think about coming here and joining the leadership team. Dive into the prayer room, and also help in outreach and other leadership areas. I think it would be great."

That was the extent of the pitch. There was no money involved, because everyone on Mike's staff is a missionary—they raise their own support. There was no pressure. Mike knew that we had a lot in Cincinnati and didn't want to be the reason that we walked away from it. He was clearly laying out an invitation, but leaving the decision to us and the Lord.

Almost as quickly as the meeting had begun, it was over. Mike got up to refill his coffee and head off to another prayer meeting. We were left sitting with his assistant, Anne. My head was spinning at the possibility of being part of something that felt so revolutionary. I looked at my wife and knew full well that her heart was already here. With my mind racing, I asked Anne, "What does he want us to do?"

She laughed, "He wants you to hear from God. But he's asking if you want to move here and join the leadership team."

Strange. That's what it had sounded like to me too.

Mike returned to the table for just a moment before he left the coffee shop. At first I thought he'd forgotten to tell Anne something. Instead, he looked right at Kelsey and me. He said, "I don't say this very often, but I'm going to. I kinda think you're moving here. I'm not telling you to. I'm just saying that I think it's going to happen." With that, he turned and walked out.

I looked at Anne. She grinned and said, "He doesn't say that too often. But when he does, he's usually right."

NINETEEN

Invited to a Classroom

—m—

W e spent most of that day driving around Kansas City. We looked at houses. We talked. We looked at schools. We talked. We went to the prayer room. We left for coffee and talked some more.

The question, of course, was about moving. It seemed illogical. I loved my role at The Vineyard. I was seeing great favor there, speaking on weekends occasionally and really enjoying my team. At times, I'd even felt like I knew what I was doing. To leave a position like that—and the security that came with a regular salary – seemed foolhardy.

Additionally, we loved Cincinnati. It was, of course, Kelsey's. In the years we'd spent there, it had become mine too. Who on earth would want to move to Kansas City?

All the while, we kept driving, talking, and thinking. By early that evening, we found ourselves in Target, wandering the aisles. We were standing before a display of soup when I looked at Kelsey and said, "We're going to do this, aren't we?"

She looked back at me and said, "Yes, I think we are."

That was the extent of our decision. It felt as if we'd been circling a drain all day and we'd suddenly gone down it. We didn't exactly know how or when, but we were certain we were going to do this. As certain as gravity.

We drove back to Aaron's house where we were staying. When we arrived, he told us, "I invited my friend, Bob, to come over and pray for you, but he called and was too tired so he went to bed." Aaron seemed pretty disappointed about this, but I didn't give it much thought—mostly because I didn't know Bob Hartley's reputation as a prophetic voice.

At 9 p.m., the phone rang. Aaron answered it and said, "Uh, yes...he is." He paused, then said, "Okay, we'll see you in a bit." He hung up and told me, "That was Bob. Bob said he fell asleep and had a dream about you. He wondered if you were bald. When I told him you were, he said he'd be right over. He has some things to tell you."

Fifteen minutes later, Bob ambled through the front door with a large sheaf of papers under his arm. He took one look at me and announced, "Yep, that's him just like in the dream." Then he looked at Kelsey and admitted, "Her hair was a different color, but that's certainly her." I was more than startled. I'm not sure what I would have done, however, had he said, "Uh, nevermind, wrong guy."

With little introduction, he sat us down on the couch, opened the file and started to talk to us.

For six months prior to that day, Bob had been having dreams that he believed were about us. He began relaying the dreams to us, describing what he saw with little interpretation. Often they were very personal scenes to us that no other person would have known if God had not revealed them to him—things like our giving a specific person money when no one was around or about great losses that we had suffered.

At this point we had not talked with Bob about our moving to Kansas City. He looked at us and said, "You are being invited here. For you, it is a classroom, and you belong in it. This is why..." and he launched into another series of stories primarily about our past.

He went on to say that many would wonder what we were doing in this classroom, but that we clearly belonged here.

It was like watching someone have a stream of consciousness download, except that every five minutes, he'd weave in a story that no other human being could know other than Kelsey and I, and each story kept coming back to us being invited into a classroom in Kansas City. Then, almost as quickly as he arrived, he announced that he was tired and needed to go home. Later we would learn that in addition to a large number of ministry commitments, Bob owned a large cleaning service that he liked to jokingly refer to as his "janitorial empire." He would often work both days and nights to keep everything running smoothly. For him to get up out of bed to drive several miles to pray for someone was not out of his character, but it certainly cost him something that it might not cost someone else.

When he left, we sat in stunned silence. Aaron took a seat in an overstuffed chair and grinned. Through his heavy New Zealand accent, he asked, "So, what do you think?"

"I think we're moving to Kansas City," was all I could muster. I've often thought how kind the Lord was in holding this experience until after Kelsey and I had agreed we were going to move. If it had happened a few hours earlier, we later might be able to discount it as manipulative. In His wisdom, God allowed us to hear His voice for ourselves, and then give us this experience as a confirmation of what we had decided for ourselves, there in the soup aisle of Target.

The next morning, we sent word through Anne, Mike's assistant, that we had made a decision and that we intended on moving as soon as practical, although that may be several months as we had a house to sell and funds to raise. Later that morning, Mike Bickle took a few more minutes with us.

Mike smiled broadly and said, "I knew it! I just sort of figured it would happen!" He went on to assure us that he was not speaking on behalf of the Lord, but on what he referred to as a holy hunch. His holy hunch was right.

Driving back to Cincinnati, I was plagued with concern. I didn't know how we'd sell our house. I wasn't sure how I could leave The Vineyard. I worried about how our boys would respond. What I didn't do was doubt. The Lord, in His graciousness, had made His plan clear. Forced to choose between clarity and ease, I would have chosen clarity again any day. As difficult as the days to come would be, we didn't deal with the doubt that we might have had if the Lord had not spoken so clearly to us.

In some ways, resigning from The Vineyard was as difficult as resigning from SpiritLife. For one thing, as hard as it is to walk away from what feels like failure, it's doubly hard to walk away from what could be perceived as success. My time at The Vineyard had been good for my heart as I learned that perhaps not all my ideas were bad, that God was not done with me, and that I could hear His voice. I also deeply enjoyed my duties there and the team I was honored to serve with.

It can almost be called a certainty that once you hear from the Lord, reasonable voices will arise to make you wonder if you're doing the right thing. Specifically, I had two pastor friends who implored me to reconsider. One of them was a fellow Vineyard staffer whose role was roughly on par with mine in the org chart. We had never been particularly close friends because both of us had busy schedules and our paths simply didn't cross, but when he learned we were leaving The Vineyard to be missionaries in a prayer movement, he felt compelled to sit me down.

"Tell me why you're doing this?" he insisted.

"Short version, I believe the Lord has told us to." There were other reasons, but this was the main one. Once you hear from the Lord, you've got to unbelieve what you heard in order to live with yourself if you fail to obey. It was easier to go forward than it was to go back.

I quickly realized that he was genuinely concerned, as he pressed, "I think this is a bad idea...I don't see how this works economically and I am concerned for your family."

Given the casual nature of our friendship, I deeply appreciated his sentiment. I didn't feel like I was being scolded or questioned, only that someone was concerned for me. Even so, I had no misgivings about our decision.

I answered, "Honestly, two weeks ago, I loved what I was doing here. It was the most exciting, fulfilling thing I could imagine. But the moment Kelsey and I admitted to one another that we thought the Lord wanted us to move, my entire role became insanely boring. It's as if the Lord lifted any desire to do it. Right now, all I can think about is what He's asked us to do."

"It scares me," he countered.

"I am grateful for your concern. Seriously, I am," I replied, "but I can handle doing without money. I can handle financial hardship if that is what the Lord brings. What I cannot bear is the idea that my children will grow up and say, 'Mom and Dad always played it safe.' I want to raise kids who will say, 'Maybe we didn't have much, but Mom and Dad would act on whatever they felt the Lord was asking them to do.'"

There were a few weeks left in the school year when we set our target for leaving Kansas City in August. That gave us the summer to sell our house, pack our belongings, and raise more money than we had ever seen in our lives. Our financial story had been one of a slow but steady trickle. Facing the fact that the trickle was about to dry up was sobering. With the help of dear friends, we made a plan for presenting our missions need to others that involved a series of small gatherings in people's homes. A few days before we started this series of meetings, I was nearly sick with dread. In retrospect, it was a bad case of what Sjogren often referred to as "fear of not enough."

I was still on staff at The Vineyard, wrapping up my duties and preparing to hand my role off to others. One day I drove home from the office worrying, which was quickly becoming my default mode. Nearing the house, I noticed something stuck against the garage door. I couldn't make it out from the street, but as I pulled into the driveway, I saw that it was green in color...as in, the color of money. It wasn't simply the color of money—it really was money.

I jumped from the truck almost before it stopped, running to the garage door where a strong wind from the east was holding four $1 bills against the garage, one on top of the other. I wasn't sure where they came from, but given the wind that day they could have been from a hundred miles away. I grabbed the four crisp bills and walked into the house.

Inside the house, I was greeted by my three sons, then ten, six, and two years old. Noting a teaching moment, and knowing that $4 wasn't going to change my world, I told the boys the story. I then told them what Kelsey and I had heard from God over the years and had reinforced by our time at The Vineyard—that if one held loosely to what God gave them, there would always be more. With that, I handed each boy a dollar and stuck the fourth in my pocket, feeling like we'd had a real My Three Sons moment. I didn't realize that the Lord was orchestrating all of this for me.

A few minutes later, Kelsey asked if I would take the trash out. I grabbed the bag and carried it out the front door to the trash can that sat near the garage. When I rounded the corner, the wind hit me full in the face. As I reached the garage door, I noticed something where the money had been found. There, were I had found $4 a few moments ago, was a crisp, new $10 bill in their place. It was as if God was laughing. He enjoyed that I'd taken a moment to teach my sons, and now He was teaching His.

Our fundraising started slowly. We were trying to raise enough to move and live on—in monthly pledges or one time gifts. We were talking thousands, not hundreds. At the rate it took us to gather the first $1,000, I imagined we'd be ready to move to Kansas City after a few years, not the months we'd planned.

We had about $1,100 in our stash when we both felt the Lord speak to us about giving $1,000 to a missionary. As scary as it was to empty our fund almost to zero, the Lord had been gracious enough to speak to both of us, so if we were going to go broke, we were going broke together. I quickly took the missionary a check before we came to our senses. They were as stunned to receive it as we had been asked to give it, but driving away, I knew beyond all shadow of a doubt that we'd heard from the Lord.

The next morning I had a meeting with one of the church planters we had coached. His church was well on its way but we would still meet regularly to discuss leadership issues and pray together. At the close of our meeting, he surprised me by saying, "I've talked to our leadership team. We want to give a significant amount to your efforts." With that, he pledged over $5,000 to us to be given over the next year.

At the end of the meeting, I sat in my truck in the parking lot and laughed at God's intricate sense of humor. I felt I'd been teaching my kids about generosity when really, God had been teaching me all along. My giving away the first few dollars that blew against the garage door had resulted in a small windfall. We were now learning that God's principles of giving work on the larger scale as well if you hold loosely to what God provides. In a measure, He was challenging my fear of not enough.

Our fundraising meetings were small affairs. We would gather for coffee and dessert at a host home, where the host had invited several couples to hear what we were going to do as prayer missionaries and then be invited to partner with us. The first meeting, a test run, was held in our home and went miserably. We did things as wrong as we could have. The meeting was too large, too crowded and too chaotic. I stammered over my words, was constantly distracted, and generally did a horrible job of presenting the opportunity. The group was full of people who were predisposed to help us and when the hat was passed, almost no one responded. It was miserable.

After the meeting, I was ready to quit. If I couldn't raise funds here, among friends, how would it work with strangers? The lessons I'd learned about God's provision were dissipating in the face of personal humiliation. Kelsey, though less discouraged than I, felt nearly as bad. Everyone left except for two dear friends whom I assumed were staying to console us. When the door shut on the last guest, the four of us stood in our foyer and they announced that we were going to debrief about the evening.

"I don't want to debrief," I said flatly.

"No," they pressed, "we need to do it now while our memory is fresh."

My fresh memory made me want to jump in front of a truck. "No," I said, "Please...go. This was awful."

Instead, they sat down at the dining room table. Against my will, but for my good, they dissected the night to determine what worked (not much) and what didn't (almost everything). Based on their good input and insistence that we talk it through, we walked away from the table not only with a belief that we had to do better, but a plan on how we could do better. Thanks to their insight, none of the other nine meetings were nearly as bad.

In thirty days of intense meetings, we had over six months of our budget in hand. The night that I realized this, I laid in bed and laughed at the goodness of God in the face of our own inability. He truly is strong when we are weak. I was realizing that this was the overwhelming truth of our life. No matter what He called us to, no matter how unprepared we were, the simple yes in our spirit would give Him just enough room to maneuver things on our behalf.

By August, we had sold our home in Cincinnati and rented one in Kansas City. We had raised a significant amount of money to get us started as missionaries. We had begun a journey of relying on God at a level that we had not yet experienced, and we had become convinced that it was only the beginning.

Jesus killed our church, but He did it so that we would learn to more fully lean on Him. I am not sure I would have learned to pray had I not been forced to. That said, it was several years before I fully understood that Jesus had killed my church, and that it was a good thing He did so. I was backstage at IHOP-KC as we were celebrating our seven year anniversary of 24/7 prayer. I remember realizing that it would have nearly been the seven year anniversary of our church start as well. Somehow I'd never made that connection before.

A lot had changed in those seven years. Time in the prayer room, time spent raising children, and seasons of maturing had moved me to be a different person than I was seven years before. I had a better grip on Scripture, on who God was, on who I was and what I needed to become. In that frame of mind, I ran across a brochure advertising a church planting conference.

Glancing over the brochure, I noticed that some of my contemporaries from church planting days were now the speakers. Those who were students were now teachers. I had to smile and wonder, "What if...what if SpiritLife had succeeded in the way we had hoped? Would that be my platform now?"

As clearly as I've ever heard His voice—not audibly, but inwardly—I heard the Lord say, "If you had been successful based on what you knew in that season, you would now be preaching that as the path to success and leading others to make the same mistakes you made. I liked your church. I killed it so you would grow into My ultimate plan for you."

Jesus killed my church. He did it for me, and I'm finally grateful He did.

TWENTY

The Take-Aways

Having finished the story of how Jesus killed my church and my coming to terms with it, I feel compelled to give a few specific take-aways. The writer in me thinks that they are points that were obviously made within the manuscript. The realist in me knows enough to spell them out. The writer in me and the realist in me occasionally get into spats, by the way.

Lest you finish reading this and wonder, "What was that all about?" here are a few things to consider:

I don't think we missed God in planting a church.

It's common to think that when things work out smoothly, the Lord was clearly in it, and when things come to a fiery ending that perhaps you made a mistake. I fully believe the Lord spoke to us, I fully believe we did what He asked, and I fully believe He brought that season to a close.

To live in a world where anything less than a smashing success is to be deemed of the devil is to live paralyzed, unable to act for fear that people will think you're manifesting a demon if you fail. If God is honored in the doing, then God is honored in the result, be it a flourishing, long-standing entity or something that comes to a close. I might feel differently if we'd left a swath of church members angry at us or God, but we didn't. The ministry of SpiritLife was valid, important, and short-lived. There is no contradiction there.

I do think I learned more than anyone I was leading.

Most leaders would say this to be true, but don't think they necessarily believe it in their heart. There is something intoxicating to the human soul to be in front of people, expected to have the answers, and deliver them, even with mixed results. Many people become leaders out of calling, but just as many out of their own want to be one. Most of us move back and forth between those two groups. I know I did. And probably do.

That said, it's not hard for me to believe that the church plant was a large construct of God to break me. Up until that point, I'd never hurt more, felt more, prayed more or trusted more than I did through that season and beyond. These are lessons I draw from every day.

Nearly a decade removed, I see my own errors with more clarity than I did even five years ago.

I've grown to believe that just as you can more easily describe an elephant from thirty feet away as you can from three feet away, you can probably better interpret your own experience ten years after the fact than you can in the midst of it.

Even in writing this, I found myself shaking my head at my own wrong thinking, my own assumptions, and my own behavior. At no point during the living through it did I think I was off base, but given the gift of perspective, it's almost comical.

I want to live life with the full understanding that over time, I will be harder on myself than on those around me. I don't want to have to wait that long to see things clearly. I want to start measuring the now by that standard. It will save me time and pain and teach me more about grace.

God's purposes really do work toward good.

Most of us do not believe this—or if we do, we don't align our minds with what we believe. Even though our heart believes in an omnipotent God with a benevolent Spirit, our own heart remains guarded, anticipating hurt and even a bad outcome from His leading.

I wish I had trusted more, leaned in farther, prayed harder, and enjoyed His hand at work even when it was doing things that seemed counter to mine.

Ten years later, I am more pleased than ever to be part of a prayer movement that I would never have embraced, had He allowed me to taste a measure of what I expected would be success as a church planter.

I look at the journey now and agree, "Just and true are all Your ways, oh Lord."

ABOUT THE AUTHOR

Randy Bohlender and his wife, Kelsey, live in Kansas City, Missouri, with their nine children.

Randy is a missionary at the International House of Prayer in Kansas City, gives direction to The Zoe Foundation and Hannah's Dream Adoptions, hosts "The Spirit of Adoption" show on Saturday mornings (730 WTNT in Washington, DC), and "The Daily Short(s)" podcast Monday through Friday.

As missionaries, the Bohlender's primary source of income comes from donations by people like you who have been touched by their message. You can find more information on how to donate under the DONATE section at www.RandyBohlender.com.

Randy is also available for speaking engagements. Inquiries can be sent to randy@thezoefoundation.com.

Other Resources

- Audio Book version of *Jesus Killed My Church*
  Available at www.JesusKilledMyChurch.com

- *The Spirit of Adoption* by Randy & Kelsey Bohlender
  Available at www.TheZoeFoundation.com

- Podcasting at www.SpiritOfAdoption.net

In the right hands, This Book will Change Lives!

Most of the people who need this message will not be looking for this book. To change their lives, you need to put a copy of this book in their hands.

> *But others (seeds) fell into good ground, and brought forth fruit, some a hundred-fold, some sixty-fold, some thirty-fold* (Matthew 13:8).

Our ministry is constantly seeking methods to find the good ground, the people who need this anointed message to change their lives. Will you help us reach these people?

> *Remember this—a farmer who plants only a few seeds will get a small crop. But the one who plants generously will get a generous crop* (2 Corinthians 9:6).

EXTEND THIS MINISTRY BY SOWING
3 BOOKS, 5 BOOKS, 10 BOOKS, OR MORE TODAY,
AND BECOME A LIFE CHANGER!

Thank you,

Don Nori Sr., Founder
Destiny Image
Since 1982